Holding My Breath

Holding My Breath
Further exploits of an ER doctor

ANNE BICCARD

First published in by Jacana Media in 2022
10 Orange Street
Sunnyside
Auckland Park 2092
South Africa
+2711 628 3200
www.jacana.co.za

© Anne Biccard, 2022

All rights reserved.

ISBN 978-1-4314-3236-3

Cover design by The Curators
Editing by Lara Jacob
Proofreading by Megan Mance
Set in Ehrhardt MT Std 12/16pt
Printed by ABC Press, Cape Town
Job no. 003889

See a complete list of Jacana titles at www.jacana.co.za

For the Blu Snoopy

Rest in peace, beautiful boy

One

5 August 2020

It is six in the morning, and I am at my post. I do not know you yet, but I am prepared for your arrival. I have practised my skills to secure your airway. I have checked my ventilator and memorised the algorithms to shock your heart. I have a list of specialists on call should I need their help. I am wearing clean scrubs and have my pen and my stethoscope at the ready.

Chances are that when you woke up today, you did not anticipate paying me a visit. Coming here is almost always a grudge purchase, and many people are resentful despite my best efforts.

Heroically, I am consulting with a little boy who has a piece of Lego stuck in his nose.

'What if it goes deeper?' Dad asks, as terrified as the boy.

'Deeper where?' I ask.

'Like into his brain or sinuses?'

Yes ... the fear is palpable.

'That won't happen,' I reassure them. 'If it is a battery, then it must come out as a matter of urgency, otherwise it will start to corrode the nostril lining. Anything else, if we can't get it out in the emergency department, or ED, we will send you to an ENT. No rush. But let's have a look.'

I am unhooking the light from the bracket on the wall when

I hear a man grunting in pain. He staggers through the double doors, hands on his chest.

'Get me a cardiologist,' he manages, his face contorted.

Here comes trouble, I think.

'Excuse me,' I say to the boy and his father, 'I need to see this patient.'

'Of course,' the father says, his eyes wide. Even the little boy, who was crying in anticipation of minor surgery, is stilled.

The guy with the chest pain looks like an owl, with a lean face and a tuft of grey hair above each ear. We get him on the bed and the sister does an electrocardiogram or ECG while I put up a drip and ask the history. No question, the Owl is having a massive heart attack. I can see it on the monitor before the print-out is done.

He tells me that he had a previous heart attack and that the pain feels the same. He confesses that he stopped taking all his chronic medication years ago but that he did take Viagra last night.

I have my heart attack protocol smoothly organised. Photograph of the ECG to the cardiologist, followed by name and age, followed closely by a call. From this point, the paths diverge, depending on the cardiologist. Amazingly, they all have different protocols, with some giving four or five different medications and holding the patient in ED, to others who literally run to the catheterisation lab without further ado.

The cardiologist today is one of the latter. She is a tiny lady with a booming voice, and she answers my call on the first ring. She gives me a few instructions but, essentially, she wants to open the vessel with a stent. The only drug she wants me to give is an infusion of isosorbide dinitrate, which will buy time by dilating the arteries to the heart. I can barely hear her with the commotion in the room and so I step outside. The wife of the Owl is pacing the corridor. I have already told her that he is having a heart attack and she looks suitably concerned.

'I can't give the isosorbide,' I tell the cardiologist. 'He had Viagra last night.'

The two drugs cannot be used together.

'Damn,' she replies. 'What time did he take Viagra? If it is more than twelve hours, then we will be okay.'

I put my hand over my mobile and ask Mrs Owl, 'What time did he take Viagra?'

She looks totally perplexed and asks, 'What Viagra?'

At the risk of her thinking me a complete moron, I say, 'Never mind, wrong patient', and hustle back into the resuscitation room. The Owl tells me that he took Viagra before seven in the evening. More than twelve hours have passed, so we start the infusion and package him off to the catheterisation lab. Time is of the essence, and I don't have a good feeling about this guy.

I go back to the Lego in the nostril. The boy starts to cry again as soon as I reappear. I suppose that I look monstrous in my mask and visor.

'I'm sorry,' he gasps between sobs, which really wrenches my heart. His nose is bleeding from where his parents have already attempted salvage.

I shine my light up his nose and see the pink Lego nestled just out of reach.

'Okay buddy, I am going to tickle the inside of your nose with this bit of plastic.' I show him a narrow suction tube. 'It won't be sore, but I need you to make your nostrils as wide as you can.'

If he can make his nostrils as wide as his eyes, this will be a walk in the park. I advance the suction up his nostril until the tip is touching the Lego, and then I close the hole on the side, making a vacuum.

'Good!' I tell him. 'Wide; wide as you can.'

The little boy flares his nostrils like a racehorse and the pink Lego sticks to the tip of the catheter and is drawn downwards.

'Got it!'

Simultaneously the boy bursts into delighted laughter and dad is moved to tears. I pat him on the shoulder, feeling a bit awkward, and high-five the boy.

Two

1 September 2020

There is the faint scent of spring in the air. The hospital is long and squat, stretched out lazily in the early light. The linoleum floor has been polished to a mirror finish overnight and the benches worn smooth by the shuffling human tide. The windows are tall and thoughtful and dipped clean in the dawn.

The first customer today reports that, the previous night, his right nipple had moved away from its usual location. He noticed its absence when he looked in the mirror and later found it in his armpit.

'Wow,' I say with a slight frown. I have never heard of a migrating nipple before. 'Let's have a look.' I slide the door shut and motion to him to pull his T-shirt off.

'Oh, it has moved back now,' he says. He takes off his shirt and I examine his chest. I even listen to his heart and lungs for good measure. Then I shake my head.

'Are you taking any recreational drugs?'

He averts his eyes. 'Crystal meth,' he confesses.

While many drugs like opium, cannabis and cocaine were originally isolated from plants, methamphetamine is synthetically produced. Both cocaine and methamphetamine are powerful stimulants, changing neurotransmitters in the brain and resulting in psychological and physical euphoria. Methamphetamine is sold in a powder or crystal form, giving it the street name crystal meth, speed or tik. It is much cheaper than cocaine and it is horribly addictive. It is sold in straws and a hit will cost you less than a takeaway coffee in South Africa. The powder can be snorted, swallowed, smoked or injected. Smoking is seemingly a popular route of ingestion, with addicts removing the metal element from light bulbs, putting the powder inside the globe, and lighting it. Apparently, the powder makes a 'tuk tuk' sound as it burns inside the glass sphere.

Stolen light fittings and globes from buildings and cars is a sure sign that tik users are coming soon to an ED near you.

Unfortunately, the methamphetamine, which is harmful enough on its own, is usually cut with poisons like battery acid, drain cleaner or antifreeze. All these toxic chemicals add up and can result in the most bizarre constellation of symptoms.

A migrating nipple is the least of his worries. But I cannot convince him that the crystal meth is the reason for what must have been a visual hallucination. He insists on blood tests and an x-ray to rule out any serious illness. He has been using drugs for years, he says, and his nipples have never moved.

I must try very hard not to roll my eyes and shake him by the scruff of his neck.

I take blood and send him for an x-ray. The results are surprisingly normal; his body is holding up well despite the abuse. It won't last, cautions the Mother Grundy in me. I can see that I am wasting my breath, but I feel that I have to say it.

It is a beautiful day outside and I can't wait to get home to the snoopies. The snoopies are a pack of rescued greyhounds, named unwittingly by a petrol attendant who saw one in the back of my car and commented on the 'beautiful Snoopy'. They have long noses and whippy tails, and they are named for the colour of the collar that they wear.

There is at least one for each shade of the rainbow.

The good thing about starting early is that I can get out of the ED by mid-afternoon. Our little pack of greyhounds has grown, with the addition of Tiger, a greyhound puppy with fitting black and brindle stripes, as well as Pookie, a tiny Pitbull rescued from a fighting syndicate.

Tiger is lanky and Pookie is squat, but both have velvety fur and sleep in a multicoloured heap, curled into each other for comfort. Pookie has a rich caramel coat, blue-green eyes, and makes the most delightful 'rrrooooo' sound when he greets. I think about him while I make a cup of tea. I hope that the gentle nature of the farm and the greyhounds will win out over his genetic fighting instinct.

Time will tell.

The next patient is a young woman who was diagnosed with colon cancer shortly after her thirtieth birthday. As it happened, I was the doctor who saw her when she first presented, and I recall her well. She had her colon removed a year ago and underwent intensive chemotherapy. Today she comes to the ED with severe abdominal pain. After conferring with the oncologist, I send her for a CT scan, and we see that the cancer has returned with a vengeance. It has spread to her liver, her lungs and her spine.

'There is nothing more to be done,' the oncologist tells me tersely. But, of course, there is always something to be done. Even though we can't treat the cancer, we can still treat the patient.

Morphine will be her new best friend. I write it up with a generous hand.

I go out to the shirking wall and sit in the sun for a minute to recalibrate and to thank the Universe for my good health. The shirking wall is a small brick retainer outside the ED, which used to be a perch for smokers. Now that smoking is more strenuously outlawed, I sometimes colonise the wall to catch a few rays and escape the windowless ED. It has a fine view of the ambulance bay, the cark park and even a manicured patch of lawn.

I see Crystal Nipple smoking in the carpark, and he gives me a death stare. I wave merrily.

I must be squirted with sanitiser when I come back through the double doors. I accept the pungent dousing without argument; after all, I can't see the naked bones in my hands yet.

Covid-19, my most recent adversary, is still lurking everywhere. We may be into our second wave of infection, or perhaps it is still the first wave, but the numbers are undulating.

The one thing that all the sanitising and mask-wearing has changed is the amount of influenza that we are seeing in the ED. Usually, winter months are packed with viral upper respiratory tract infections. Maybe people are still getting them but are too afraid to come to the hospital. There is Coro Coro here.

The next patient is a case in point. Seventy years old, with underlying diabetes and high blood pressure, he is coughing and has a high fever. He is from North India and does not speak English at all, but he is accompanied by a very articulate and concerned family.

I take blood and do a chest x-ray and see coronavirus infection on the films and results. There are far fewer positive cases now, but three or four still trickle in daily.

The angry white clouds on the x-ray are so typical, blotting out the lung tissue. We swab the patient for the virus, and I call the family in.

'His diabetes is out of control. His sugar is very high, and his blood is becoming acidic.' I show them the results. 'Also of concern is that he is very dehydrated, his oxygenation is poor, and his electrolytes are dangerously deranged.'

They look at me with liquid eyes above their beautifully coloured outfits.

'And his chest x-ray looks terrible.' I show them the film, but I guess that they don't know what a normal chest x-ray looks like. 'He has bad pneumonia; I am pretty sure it is coronavirus.'

'But you don't have the test result yet?' the oldest brother asks.

'No. The swab result will only be ready tomorrow. But based

on the x-ray and the blood results that we have so far, I am sure it is corona.'

The brother holds up his hand, as if warding off an evil wish that I am trying to cast on them.

'We will wait for the result,' the family group all nod in unison.

'OK, we will let you know as soon as we have it,' I assure them, 'but he will need to be admitted to the Person Under Investigation or PUI ward.'

'Admitted?' The brother looks horrified and his eyes double in size. 'To the hospital?'

'Yes.' I say and repeat all the reasons that I want him to stay.

'Oh no, but doctor, he might get coronavirus in the hospital.'

'I'm pretty sure that he already has corona,' I repeat.

'Ha, doctor's sense of humour,' the second brother interjects, and they all laugh along.

'I'm not joking,' I say. 'I know that I don't have the swab result, but I have seen a lot of Covid pneumonias over the past six months. I recognise it.'

Try as I might, I cannot convince the family that their father should be admitted. It is difficult, as I try to get them to translate for me, but I suspect that there are important bits of information that are being missed out along the way. I need to ensure that the patient himself understands the situation fully and this is impossible if the translators have their own agenda.

After a good half an hour of brisk debate, the family and the patient sign a document called a Refusal of Hospital Treatment. The RHT has an area that I can fill in, clearly stating my advice, the reasons therefore, and the possible consequences of refusal. There is also a large disclaimer at the bottom of the form which tells the patient that the facility has the right to refuse further treatment should they come back. I always go through the paperwork carefully with them and make sure that they understand that they are welcome to come back at any time.

I give the patient as much fluid as I can over the following hour, correct his sugar and electrolytes to the best of my ability, and let him go home.

The next day I call one of the sons to tell him that the swab for coronavirus is positive. It doesn't sound like he believes me. I ask him how his dad is doing.

'Oh, he is much worse, doctor.'

'Worse?' I ask with alarm.

'Oh yes. He can hardly breathe at all now.'

'Well, you must bring him back. Straight into Covid ICU.' I shake my head and make the arrangements.

Three

Crystal Nipple is back. This time he has gone too far, and he is soundly unconscious. I rub his sternum and shout his name. His nipples are in place, and I tweak them to try and wake him up. No luck. When I lift his eyelids, his left eye is gazing off to the side and his right is staring straight ahead. His pupils are like matt saucers; they take up his whole iris, leaving only a rim of blue. It is creepy to think of pupils as apertures; holes into which I might fall.

'Divergent gaze,' I jot in my mental notes. 'Glasgow Coma Scale three out of fifteen. Pupils dilated and unresponsive to light.'

His breathing is erratic and with his decreased level of consciousness, he will need to be intubated and put on a ventilator. He is sharing the resuscitation room with a middle-aged man who has chest pain. Mr Chest Pain looks a bit young to be having a heart attack, but I hear him telling the sister earnestly that he thinks he is having one. I dart between the two beds, setting Crystal Nipple up for intubation and getting a basic history from Chest Pain.

'Hi. Can you tell me about the chest pain?'

'I think I am having a heart attack.'

'How old are you?'

'Thirty-five.'

'When did the pain start, where is it and how much out of ten?'

'It is eleven out of ten, right here in the middle of my chest and it goes down both of my arms. Been there for about an hour.'

'Do you have any other medical history?'

'Nope.'

'Nothing? No chronic medication, history of heart disease, smoker?'

I know that I am rushing through his history, but I need to get back to Crystal. I can see his saturation is bobbing around the 90 per cent mark, and I cannot wait too long to secure his airway.

'Nope.'

'Well, it would be unusual for an otherwise healthy thirty-five-year-old to be having a heart attack, but nothing is impossible. We are going to do an ECG and take some blood. I will be attending to the guy in the next cubicle, and I will come and chat to you soon.'

While I get ready to intubate Crystal, I eyeball the ECG scrolling out of the machine next to me and I see that Chest Pain is, indeed, having a heart attack.

Excellent. Now there are two life-threatening events happening concurrently. At least they are in adjacent beds.

Crystal is so deeply unconscious that I don't need to sedate him. I just open his mouth with a piece of equipment called a laryngoscope, shine a light down his throat and guide the plastic tube through his vocal cords. It sounds so simple, but there is always a little tension around intubation. It can be easy – and it can be well nigh impossible. And if it turns out to be a difficult one, the ED doctor has a problem on her hands. Especially if she has paralysed a patient who was previously breathing for themselves.

Without sedation, the patient struggles and retches and there is almost no chance of the tube ending up in the correct place. But once you sedate and paralyse a person who was breathing when they arrived in the ED, you had better be able to take those functions over efficiently. And you only have thirty seconds or so before the oxygen saturation in their blood starts to drop. Another minute or so and their heart will stop due to lack of oxygen.

Cardiac arrest from poor oxygenation in a patient that was

previously breathing on their own is a very bad thing.

Since Crystal has sedated himself, it takes a bit of pressure off me. Luckily, he has an easy airway – a big mouth and a small tongue and his larynx is well-positioned – and so we are OK. I set up the ventilator and order blood tests and then scoot over to Chest Pain and have a proper look at his ECG. He watches my face like a hawk.

'I am having a heart attack, aren't I?'

I raise my eyebrows and scratch my ear. 'Yep, it does look like it.'

'I knew it!' He sounds almost victorious. I feel like he might fist-pump the air.

It is a strange thing that some patients almost want to have something wrong with them. If all the tests come back normal, they are slightly crestfallen. Except for coronavirus. No one wants to hear that the swab was positive. Partly because of the stigma, but I think that the big fear is the unpredictability of the illness to come.

Patients often think that a bone is broken and seem disappointed when the x-ray is normal. I suppose that it is a good war story, to tell of serious injury, but in general the inconvenience of a fracture far outweighs the tale of heroism that accompanies it.

Certainly, the consequences of a heart attack in a young guy with no risk factors are arduous.

I am sometimes asked if I have checked for 'everything'. I must explain that there is no blood test for 'everything'. You must choose what you are testing for, and why. The answer is only as thorough as the question asked. I am reminded of the Peter Sellers movie when he asks, 'Does your dog bite?' 'No,' replies the elderly man. As Sellers bends to greet the dog, it bites him and the man adds, 'That is not my dog.'

It is all about the question.

The snoopies and Pookie the velvet brick are waiting for their walk when I get home. The sun is slanting, and it is the magical time when the world seems suspended in a golden light. The dogs stack up at the gate and flood through as it opens, the greyhounds bounding gracefully in the front and Pookie barreling along at the back. I wonder if he feels envious or slow, or whether dogs are spared the painful self-reflection that haunt us humans.

I scoop up Pookie as he is lagging and the setting sun is rich red on his caramel coat. His ears stand up and the light shines through them. The skin is so thin there, ruby red and soft, and his wide adder-mouth smiles up at me.

I set him down to run once we are through the thick grass, and we follow a sandy path along the edge of the field. The grassland is purple and thick with flowers in the cool spring evening.

The acacia trees are now black against a sky full of blood; the evening star shimmering above their thick canopies. Familiar constellations appear in the midnight blue and the moon is almost full in the east. I think of the wanderers, navigating by the night lights, searching for a fixed star in their sky, a familiar road, no matter their restlessness.

The night sky is as familiar to me as my own body. Sometimes it feels so close, as if I could jump up and stretch out, on the flat edge of a half moon.

Maybe that is what happens when you die.

It is a perfect evening on this stretch of grassland, and surrounded by the snoopies and Pookie and Tiger, I say another thank you to the Universe.

Four

10 S<small>EPTEMBER</small> 2020

The waiting room is humming with customers. Now that the lockdown is lifted to stage one, numbers are up again. The doorbell chimes and the ambulances drone in and out of the bays, dropping patients for us like trussed up baskets of pollen.

The paramedics offload a frail lady who is complaining of generalised weakness. She is very personable and smiles sweetly at me while I take her history. The monitor above her head registers her systolic blood pressure as sixty millimetres of mercury. The machine squarks in fright and immediately starts to re-inflate the cuff. The second reading is fifty. I glance at it in concern. No wonder she is feeling weak; that blood pressure is less than a third of what it should be.

Granny is ninety years of age this year and is a heavy smoker. Other than that, she is in excellent health. She started feeling weak this morning and she feels dizzy if she stands up. She has no pain at all.

'I'm sure it's nothing serious,' she tries to reassure me.

'Mmmmm,' I say, checking her pulse and feeling her tummy. With such a low blood pressure, she must be bleeding from somewhere. I enquire again about vomiting blood or having dark stools, but she shakes her head vehemently. I do a rectal exam just to make sure. It is all clear.

I check the clock. It is just before seven in the evening and the radiologist will be packing up to go home. I call the x-ray department and, fortunately, the doctor on call takes my last-minute request seriously.

He materialises at Granny's bed within about five minutes, his sonar probe in hand. I tell him that we are looking for free fluid in her abdomen.

'Yep. Lots of free fluid,' he confirms as the grainy images swim into view.

'Ruptured aortic aneurysm?' I ask.

'I'm not sure,' he answers honestly. 'This fluid looks further forward than I would expect from the aorta, but we need to do a CT scan with contrast to be sure.' He glides his little probe up under Granny's ribs on her left. 'Where is her spleen?'

We both turn from the monitor and look at Granny.

'Where is your spleen?' I ask her.

She shrugs. 'I don't know,' she answers.

'I mean, have you had it removed?' I ask, checking her left side for a tell-tale scar.

'Not as far as I know,' she looks perplexed.

'She is bleeding from a ruptured spleen, then,' the radiologist says. 'All this fluid and no spleen visible, it has to have burst.'

'Burst?' I repeat, staring at him. 'Why would it burst?'

'Well, now, you are the clever ED doctor who is going to figure that one out.'

There is that faint crinkle of mirth at the corners of his eyes, no doubt because of my expression of complete confusion. He starts to pack up his machine. 'We can, of course, do a CT with contrast to confirm it. Let me know.'

And with that, he departs, leaving me with a spleenless Granny and a chiming monitor.

'Are you absolutely sure that you didn't fall or hurt yourself on your left side?' I ask as I prod the left side of her chest.

The ribs are a cage, protecting the vascular organs beneath, and they would usually break before a deeper structure is damaged. Trauma is about the only reason for a ruptured spleen that I can think of in an elderly patient with no other illnesses.

'Definitely not.' Granny is still sharp as a tack. She also has absolutely no pain over her ribs.

'Huh,' I say, and dial the surgeon on call. I can hear that he is as skeptical of a spontaneously ruptured spleen in a ninety-year-old as I am. He is not going to risk taking her for surgery until we are sure, so we send Granny for the CT with contrast.

In the meantime, I start replacing some of the fluid that she has lost. I must go carefully as she seems to have reached some equilibrium. If I push her blood pressure up too much, it will make her bleed more. I need to give her just enough to keep her vital organs perfused and to keep her conscious.

I find her family in the waiting room and update them. Her daughter tells me that there is absolutely no way her mother can have an operation. Her lung function is terrible from all the smoking, and she will not survive an anaesthetic.

'If her spleen is ruptured, we are going to have to take that chance,' I tell them. 'We can't just let her die.'

The family looks startled at the bluntness of my statement, but it is the truth and there is no time for chit chat.

The surgeon arrives in the ED as Granny returns from x-rays. He seems bothered, pacing around and flapping at imaginary flies. He examines Granny and looks at the scans. He chases a few more invisible things from around his head and I wonder if it is his thoughts that are buzzing in his ears.

I have presented the findings to him and now he must decide. I stand quietly, trying not to hype the moment or put him under pressure. It is a very unusual case, and he is, after all, the specialist surgeon. It takes him about thirty seconds, but he reaches the same conclusion as I have.

'We must take her immediately to the theatre.'

Once the decision is made, frantic activity is loosed in the ED. Admission documents, consent forms, a hospital green gown and the anaesthetist all materialise, and, within ten minutes, Granny is wheeled straight into surgery.

Her spleen was, indeed, ruptured, but fortunately the blue-eyed surgeon got the splenic artery clamped and saved day.

I visit her the next day in ICU. She recognises me and squeezes my hand. She might be ninety, but she still counts as a save from Grim. I have no idea why I persist in seeing the Grim Reaper as male in gender, and I know that he always wins the long game, but I have a running battle with him, and I chalk up every victory that I can.

Five

The red phone rings, shrill and impatient. This line is reserved for radio–landline patches from emergency personnel in the field. It seldom bodes well when it rings, bringing resuscitations and desperately ill patients to the ED. Today, paramedics are bringing an unconscious patient from her home. She is seventy years old and was found, unrousable, by her helper this morning.

There is nothing much happening in the ED this morning, so I go out and sit on the shirking wall. The early sun is warm on my back, and I feel sleepy. Within five minutes the ambulance, decorated in dayglo, reverses into the bay.

The patient looks like she, too, has spent many hours lazing in the sun. Her skin is uniformly tanned, and her hair bleached blonde. Together with obvious breast implants, she looks much younger than seventy. She looks like a pickled Barbie doll, and she is about as responsive. Shouting, tweaking and prodding solicits no response at all.

Barbie is properly unconscious.

The paramedics have no other history for me: no medical conditions, no daily medication, no known allergies. I wonder why so many unconscious people seem to be arriving in the ED recently. It is like a sardine run of semi-dead people.

I start with the basics. Check dextrose level and send blood for electrolytes, inflammatory markers, and levels of prescription medication, like sleeping tablets, that may be in her system. We do an ECG and send her down for an urgent CT scan as she may be bleeding into her brain.

While Barbie is down in x-rays, a slightly hysterical girl is hustled through the emergency entrance. The ambulance has moved, and her parents have parked their car in the bay, flashers bright in the gloom.

'Help! My daughter was struck by lightning!'

Mom is shouting while her husband carries their sobbing daughter from the car. I am surprised, as there is no sign of a storm at present, but we take the girl straight through to the resuscitation room. I have never had a lightning strike victim in the ED before, but I read up on it a few years ago after some unlucky schoolboys were struck on the cricket pitch of a private school in Johannesburg.

The literature says that a direct hit accounts for about five per cent of lightning strike injuries and is almost always fatal. Much more common is a side-splash or a ground strike, where the current runs along the ground or through the air from a nearby tree or building that is struck.

The massive current involved – approximately thirty million volts – can stop the heart and shock the medulla of the brain, halting the impulse to breathe. In lightning strikes, the heart usually resets itself before the brain, and so it is very important to start the respiratory part of CPR as soon as possible. If the patient is not ventilated, the heart will stop again from lack of oxygen.

Judging by the loud crying, this girl is certainly breathing well. From her history, it sounds like she suffered a ground strike. She was walking on a sports field and the nearby gazebo was struck by an unexpected bolt. It was a small building with a tent-like extension and the whole thing exploded. I examine her for any sign of blast injury, particularly ruptured eardrums. I also check for burns and wounds from flying fragments of gazebo. We do an ECG for rhythm abnormalities and check her blood for electrolyte abnormalities and muscle breakdown.

Everything comes back normal. Lifetime risk of being struck by lightning is about one in 15 000 and I tell her that she made a lucky escape. She looks quite pleased with herself and is already posting on social media.

Barbie is back from x-rays by now and I gather all her results together. To my surprise, they are all completely normal. Blood tests and scans are pristine. I go back to the bed and examine her again. She is like a sleeping doll, breathing well but completely unresponsive. I call for advice from the physician. He can't think of anything that I have overlooked, so he tells me to admit her to the ICU and he will review her within the hour.

When I see the physician later, I ask him what he thinks is wrong with her.

'She was a mystery until her family came in.' He confides. 'As soon as they saw me, they asked if she had started using again.'

'Using?' I ask.

'Yep. Heroin,' he replies, rolling his eyes.

'That seventy-year-old lady was using heroin?'

I am incredulous. It never even crossed my mind to check her blood or urine for recreational drugs. Which is a lesson to myself and the assumptions that I make about my patients. It would be the first test that I would run on an unconscious twenty-year-old.

In my defense, not many heroin users make it to the age of seventy.

Six

16 September 2020

The medical profession in South Africa has been rocked today by the apparent assassination of a colleague. He was shot six times and died on the scene, just a few blocks from our hospital. He was the anaesthetist in a case that went wrong about six months ago. Tragically, a child died shortly after surgery and both the anaesthetist and the paediatric surgeon faced charges. I heard, informally, that the postmortem revealed that neither was to blame for the child's death, but perhaps someone decided to take the law into their own hands.

What is the world coming to, doctors ask each other in the corridors? If a patient dies whilst under your care, is it murder? Did either of those doctors go to work that morning with evil or wrongful intent?

Maybe it was a coincidence, I hear in the tearoom. Maybe he was secretly a drug lord or owed money to the mafia. I shake my head. Crime is so rife in our country that people are routinely gunned down. But there was no robbery here; his mobile phone and wallet were untouched.

And I am pretty sure, having met him a few times, that he was not a member of the mafia.

As a group, the medical profession is divided on everything

from politics and religion to a simple diagnosis. Doctors like to think for themselves, but this makes us unable to stand together on any one issue. The assassination of a colleague is a case in point.

Trying to get any kind of protest going is like trying to herd a group of cats.

It all feels so wrong and yet it seems that there is not much that I, personally, can do about it. I feel like rebelling; sitting on the shirking wall and refusing to see any patients until the murder is solved. But that would leave a lot of innocent people badly affected, so I feel stuck and angry.

Regardless of how I feel, the files keep coming through. The administration lady has an infuriating way of flinging them into the tray from a few metres away, like paper frisbees. They land with a whoosh and slap, one on top of the other. I grit my teeth and stop myself from intercepting them. I want to seize them, mid-air, and fling them out of the window.

I try to keep my head down and get through the shift, but I am just not in the mood today. As if sensing my discontent, the sisters seem to be on a 'go-slow' and patients are presenting with the strangest ailments. The physician is annoyed with me for sending one of his patients home yesterday, although he refused to accept her, and he complains loudly to everyone who will listen.

I want to throw him out of the window too.

I am sure that there is a correlation between laziness and casting blame. There is also an inverse correlation between the length of a radiology report and how uncertain the radiologist is of the diagnosis. If there is something simple, and obvious, the report will be a few lines. But today I am getting three-page reports telling me that 'there is an impression' and 'clinical correlation is advised'.

I want to call downstairs and tell them to stop sitting on the fence. I am just grumpy, and I have pain in my back to add to my irritable mood.

Mostly I just want to go home and have a long walk on the farm with the snoopies, but there are still another four hours to go.

It feels interminable.

The sisters bring through a dapper man. He is about eighty but in excellent shape with a fine head of silver hair and freshly veneered teeth. He has a little handkerchief folded in his shirt pocket that matches his belt and shoes. He perches expectantly on the bed.

I greet him and open the front cover of the file, ready to take the history.

'Doctor,' he says earnestly, 'I hope that you know CPR.'

I look up.

'Because you take my breath away.'

He gives me a charming flash of teeth and I am speechless for a second. I doubt that he can even see me, behind all my layers of PPE, and I am certainly no oil painting.

'Please tell me that you are not married,' he continues, and he seems to be serious.

This guy, who is old enough to be my father, is flirting outrageously with me and I am not sure how to respond. I don't want to be rude, but I need to put a stop to it.

'Yes, I am married,' I lie, 'and what can I do for you today?'

He looks genuinely disappointed, but we get on with the consultation. As I escort him out of the ED, he tells me that I really am his type.

It is an uncomfortable moment, and it gets worse when a huge bouquet of flowers arrives at the front desk.

Mr Dapper appears every day thereafter in the ED. From being quaint, he is taking on the role of a proper stalker. He tells the sister at the front desk that he is here to visit me. I refuse to see him unless he is actually sick and so he opens a file. He makes up a few complaints and it becomes more and more awkward. Eventually, I must confront him.

'I am really flattered by your attention, but I need to be clear that I am not interested at all in any kind of relationship. I am very happy with my partner. I am concerned that, if you keep opening files to see me, you are going to run out of medical savings.'

He looks down and becomes suddenly tearful. It turns out that he was bereaved a few months ago and is desperately lonely. He shows me a few photographs of his wife on his mobile. She was a truly beautiful woman. He also shows me a video clip of him playing the saxophone and he is an excellent musician. He takes out his little colour-coded handkerchief and wipes his eyes. He thanks me for my time and slowly makes his way out of the ED.

I feel terrible and resist the impulse to run after him and agree to coffee. That is not the answer, I tell myself sternly. It would be unethical and counterproductive. But still, he is lonely and means no harm. I slump down on the shirking wall and stare at the shimmering green canopy over the parking area. A light breeze shuffles the leaves, and they sound like water running.

I look at the smokers, back on the job after the ban on cigarettes was lifted, haze rising from their noses and mouths like steaming dragons.

A few days later, I hear from the sisters that Mr Dapper passed away. I start feeling guilty all over again. Maybe he died of a broken heart. Maybe I should have gone to have coffee with him.

'Stop it,' I tell myself firmly. 'Get a grip.'

Seven

23 September 2020

I am really struggling to get through my shift today. I feel like there is something wrong with my vision, with dark spots swarming around. When I stand up, I feel lightheaded, and I am so tired that I could just fall asleep. When I go up to the ICU to help with a resuscitation, I glance at the reflective lift doors and barely recognise myself. I look like a ghost; my eyes are hollow and my cheeks above my mask are almost translucent. Maybe it is stress – the last few months of being pummeled by the pandemic have been beyond speech in their awfulness – but I suppose that I should do some blood tests.

Later, I think; the ED is ridiculously busy, and I am kept scurrying around all morning.

Mid-afternoon, a patient is brought by ambulance. He is complaining of chest pain, and I start to write his history in the file. My ears are blocked, and I feel very strange. There is a faint roaring sound in my head, like a distant waterfall.

It sounds dangerous.

I decide to sit down, before I fall down, and pull out the little step that the patient uses to get up on the bed. I settle on it and continue to take his history. My nose is now at the same level as his belt, and I am holding the file in my lap. If the patient thinks it strange, he doesn't say a thing. He just adjusts his position in the bed so that he can still see me, and we go on.

The ECG scrolls out of the machine, which is at my new eye-level, and I see that there are changes. I really don't feel up to managing this patient and I call the cardiologist and ask him if he can take the patient over. I tell him that I am not feeling well, and I hear concern in his voice. He comes down to the ED immediately, glancing at me over his mask and through his visor.

'You look very pale,' he observes, and asks if there is anything that he can do to assist.

I ask the laboratory to take some blood from me and then I finish up my paperwork. As I am about to leave, the senior laboratory technician comes into the tiny doctors' office. He pulls the door shut and puts the results on the table.

'Are these your results, doctor?' he asks kindly. 'I don't want to print them as…' his voice fades away. The printer is on the front desk of the ED, open to all eyes. I thank him for his discretion and glance over the results. I already have some idea about what could be wrong, but it is confirmed on the letterhead.

My haemoglobin is low. Very low; too low to even try and excuse as a variation on normal. I sigh. It is low enough to warrant a transfusion – but the worrying question is why it is so low. In the moment, I resign myself to the inescapable truth that I am going to need investigations and, probably, admission to hospital.

Maybe I am iron deficient. Maybe I am bleeding from somewhere. But, aside from the weakness and spotty vision, I have no symptoms. No pain and no obvious source of bleeding.

I call my partner, Alida, and give her a summary. She sounds worried: 'So, what does this mean?'

'I don't know,' I reply honestly. 'We will have to see what the test results show.'

And tests there are. By the dozens. Some colleagues stop by my bed and chat. Others stay away; perhaps thinking I need some privacy or prefer to hold fast to the age-old belief that doctors never get sick.

I stare out of the window, at the bleak, wind-swept parking area. This heaviness in my heart is like a stone. Unbidden, a tear trickles down my cheek.

Maybe I am depressed, I think to myself. But depression will not cause such an abnormal haemoglobin.

'Ah, doctor, don't cry.' The sister pats my arm, adjusting the drip. 'You are our doctor. Who will be looking after us all when you are sick? You will be better soon. We are all praying for you.'

She is so kind. Am I missing something as a health care provider, I wonder to myself? I don't think I am empathetic enough to the people who come through my department.

It's not so nice to be on the other side.

Eight

So far, all the tests are clear. Iron stores, B12, folate, endoscopes, CT scan with contrast – all normal. I can see something is bothering my favourite physician.

'We need to do a bone marrow biopsy,' he tells me. 'With everything else normal, we need to exclude leukaemia.'

I don't think that I have leukaemia. A cancer of the bone marrow and blood-producing cells, leukaemia would affect all the lines of cells. But I have asked him to be my physician and so I should do the investigations that he recommends.

The doctor comes to take the bone marrow. She tells me that I must inform her of any severe pain in my abdomen during the biopsy, as this will mean that she has pushed the trocar right through the bone of my pelvis. Charming, I think, and gaze up at the ceiling. Take a deep breath and remove myself mentally from the room. Channel the softness of Pookie's velvet ears.

I am sure that this severe anaemia has something to do with Covid-19. I have never been anaemic before, except for when I was shot in the chest and bled out half of my blood volume. But that was eight years ago, and my haemoglobin recovered within a few months. Now my blood has disappeared as if by a miracle. There is no sign of it, other than low red cells and very high reticulocytes.

Reticulocytes are baby red blood cells, and my body is pumping them out at full speed. Trying to replace what has been lost, my bone marrow has its foot on the gas. The question remains, where have the red cells gone?

Maybe there is a vampire in my house. I smile at the image of a greyhound, sharpening its teeth on a stone outside. I know exactly which one it would be, too. Lola, the most recent rescue, is very quick with her teeth. She was pregnant when we got her, and we chalked her snappy behaviour down to hormones and a new environment with a whole litter of pups. But the puppies are all homed, and she has been spayed. She still bites people when she can.

We had a little chat yesterday. I am sure that she will mend her ways.

My own theory is that my body attacked the red cells and burst them. Called haemolysis, it is a possible consequence of corona infection. In fact, it seems that anything can be kick-started by this virus. Dementia, Parkinson's, auto-immune diseases, diabetes, acute heart failure.

All in a day's work for Covid-19.

Nine

A few days' rest, a slightly improved red cell level, and I am back at my post.

A man is waiting in room seven. He has a translator with him, but I cannot establish the reason for the consultation. They both keep pointing to his groin and telling me there is a problem. The urine is clear. His genitals look normal on examination. He is only in his twenties so it can't be a prostate problem. We go backwards and forwards until the translator brings out a little electronic notepad and types in the wording.

The machine tells me, in a quaint English accent, that the patient has premature ejaculation.

'What does ejaculation mean?' the translator asks.

I stare at him for a long moment. How does one explain ejaculation, other than with the word 'ejaculation' or a slang term for it? He follows quickly with a request for Viagra.

This gives me an idea of how to address the problem.

'Does he have a problem making it stand up?' I ask, my hand, tilting involuntarily at the wrist to help with the imagery.

'No, no, it stands well, but he finishes too quickly, before it is even in, and then it goes down.'

'So, it is standing fine, but,' now a different hand movement, 'it happens too early?'

'Yes, yes!'

They are thrilled that I am finally getting the gist.

I try to explain to them that, once he has ejaculated, he will lose the erection, regardless of Viagra. I tell them about exercises and squeezing techniques, but a good medication is a new generation antidepressant. One of the most common side effects is delayed ejaculation.

The translator has a hundred queries about the condition and treatment. I want to bang my forehead on the table as they have a rapid, animated conversation and then roll out the questions. How long is normal intercourse? How hard should it be? How much ejaculate? Is it wrong if the semen runs out of his girlfriend when she stands up?

'No, that's gravity.' I am getting a bit impatient with this consult. 'There is nowhere else for it to go. The vagina is like the inside of a sock, not an endless pathway.'

I don't think that they like that comparison. In fact, the patient looks horrified.

'But for how long should it last? How long is normal?' The translator is taking his job very seriously.

To be honest, they could not have chosen a worse doctor to give them advice about the ins and outs of heterosexual intercourse. I have no idea of how long it should last. I side-step the issue, telling them that there is no 'normal'; if he and his partner are satisfied.

'Fifteen minutes?' The translator sounds hopeful. I tell him that seems a bit long to me and bid them farewell. I hate to cut things short, so to speak, but I have been in the room for almost half an hour and there are other patients waiting.

I catch the sister's eye as I leave the room. She tells me that intercourse shouldn't last longer than a minute. She was obviously eavesdropping, and I shake my head with a smile.

'A minute?' I ask, teasingly. The other sisters concur; after a minute he must finish up.

Interesting.

'No more sex education today,' I inform the sister on triage.

As if she has any control over who walks through the door.

Ten

The red phone summons me to a resuscitation in the ward. It is three floors up and the lift is not working. The sister and I carry the resuscitation bag between us and steam up the staircase. The bag is heavy, but we have learned that we must take everything that we might need. In a resuscitation, your equipment must be ready and right under your hand. There is no time for searching through drawers or wheeling out a machine that has not been charged.

It turns out not to be a resuscitation, but only a patient who fainted in the bathroom. Once she is revived, we are free to go. I meet up with the physician in the hallway; he was also paged for the resuscitation, but I reassure him that we are not needed. He will see her later, on his ward round, but for now he is rushing back to a sick patient in the ICU.

'You look a bit pale,' he remarks as we leave the ward.

'Yep, my haemoglobin dropped, and I am very anaemic,' I tell him.

He pauses.

'Iron levels, B12, folate?' he asks. He is an academic who usually heads a unit at a teaching hospital, but he is covering the physicians at this hospital for the weekend.

'Yes, we checked all that,' I tell him.

He looks me up and down. 'And your thyroid?' he asks.

'Yes. Why? Have I gained weight?'

He shakes his head. 'I think it's just the scrubs.'

I'm not sure if he is joking or not, but I roll my eyes. 'Really?' I ask. 'What kind of thing is that to say?'

I don't want to hold him up, but I can see that he loves puzzles. We say goodbye and he trots off down the stairs.

Two flights down, he shouts over his shoulder 'Parvovirus B19?' It echoes up the stairwell and a little bell rings in my head.

About a month before I started feeling so tired, we adopted a puppy from an animal rescue centre. They told us that the puppy was vaccinated, but a few days after she arrived, she got sick. A week later, a few thousand rand at the vet and a house full of coughing, vomiting dogs, little Addie died. She had both Parvovirus and Distemper. The greyhounds were all vaccinated, so they had a milder version.

I didn't know that humans could get Parvovirus.

Google tells me that Parvovirus is common in children. It causes a lacy, red rash that typically starts on the cheeks. It used to be the fifth most common viral cause of this kind of rash and is accordingly called 'Fifth Disease' or 'slapped cheek syndrome'. In very rare cases, and especially if there is concurrent exposure to coronavirus, it can cause the bone marrow to stop making red blood cells. This causes a severe, but transient, anaemia.

How interesting. Google is adamant that a different strain of Parvovirus infects animals and humans, but I wonder how they can be so sure of that. Perhaps they test for the different strains in humans, but I am pretty sure that it is a broad-based test in dogs.

Best I get back to work. If I leave the unit for a few minutes or get caught up in a resuscitation, I get behind the curve. All the cubicles are full, and I search around for the next patient. I have his file in my hand, but I cannot find the corresponding person. Eventually I sit down at the nurses station and wait for a sister to come along. I am still a bit breathless from my climb up the stairs.

'Hello. Do you know where this patient is?' I ask her, showing her the file.

'Ah. He is in the linen closet, doctor,' she replies smoothly.

'Excuse me?' I ask.

'The linen closet,' she repeats. 'We put him in there because there are no other beds.'

Of course, I mumble under my breath. The linen closet. What an obvious place to stash a patient. Especially an eighty-year-old with dementia. If the file went missing, and we didn't need linen, he could be stranded there for hours. Days even.

He is sitting in a wheelchair, facing a pile of towels and sheets. I prop my notes on the full basket of unwashed linen – which is mostly clean as, with corona around, we must change everything between each patient – and try to get a history. The elderly man has no idea of who he is nor why he is here, and I cannot ask a family member into the linen closet to get the history. He just clutches my arm with his cold, bony hand and holds on. I am amazed at how smooth and soft the skin on his palm is.

Defeated, I gently disengage myself, take the file back to the doctor's room and wait for a room to open so that I can move him to a bed. In the meantime, I get on with the next one.

Eleven

17 October 2020

Two hours of my shift have passed, and I have not seen one patient. I am onto my third cup of tea and have taken to prowling the corridors, looking for snacks or colleagues.

Neither is available. On a Saturday morning the hospital is deserted, and the coffee shop is not open yet.

I am bored.

I should do some internet-based learning or read up on an interesting case. There is a new diploma that Emergency Medicine doctors can write; perhaps I should enquire. I cannot seem to access a hunger for knowledge today, though, so I just cruise past the magazine rack and waste five minutes before returning to the ED.

There are some posts on our group about the Covid vaccine trials. Corona is an RNA virus, and so the vaccine will work in a different way to the vaccines that we have so far, which are all for DNA viruses. RNA is a messenger strand of genetic material that builds protein in the cell rather than in the nucleus.

DNA vaccines work by injecting little bits of dead or inactivated virus that scare up a defense from our immune system. As I understand it, RNA vaccines will cause the RNA in our own cells to make the protein, and then our immunity will build against it.

It seems a bit risky to me, to teach your cells to build a foreign protein. But the literature seems to think that it will be safer.

The doorbell at the ambulance bay entrance sounds. We used to leave these double doors unlocked, but they open directly onto the street with no security. Now, the hospital has installed a video camera to show us who is outside before we unlatch the door. There is also a massive sign that explains that this entrance is for ambulances only. The actual ED entrance is a few steps around the corner, but people still ring the bell.

I glance at the monitor and see a new model car parked across the three bays. There is a giant man glowering at the locked doors and he rings the bell twice more. I click the lock open and swing the door.

'Hello,' I say. I don't ask him if he can read, or why he is out here in the street, when there is a welcoming entrance just around the corner, with secure parking, wheelchairs, and a triage nurse, all set up for his arrival.

'My wife is sick,' he explains. I see his wife, sitting in the passenger seat. She stares at us through the windscreen.

'OK,' I say. 'Can she walk, or shall we get a wheelchair?'

The giant man shrugs, and stares at me vacantly. I hold back a sigh and walk to the car. The woman watches me approach and gazes at me through the tinted side window. She makes no move to open the door, so I try the handle.

It is locked.

I look back at the Giant and ask him to open the car. He pats his trouser pockets and shrugs again. He has left the keys in the car.

I knock on the window and make a winding motion with my hand. She stares at me, unblinking, and does not move a muscle.

The statue-like woman has locked herself in the car, with the keys in the ignition.

'What is the reason for the consultation today?' I ask the Giant.

'She has a headache. But she just wants some medication; she doesn't want to see the doctor.'

'I'm afraid that I cannot give her medication without seeing her as a patient,' I explain, and I look in at the woman again. If she were unconscious, or struggling to breathe, we would have to break the window. But she is sitting bolt upright, made up and dressed to the hilt; she is alert and doesn't look distressed at all. She is just sitting there, watching us move helplessly around the outside of the car.

An ambulance reverses towards us and blips his siren. I go and explain that we cannot move the car for now. He moves off irritably; he is going to have to offload his patient in the parking lot and push the stretcher up the hill. It is only nine in the morning, but it is already blazingly hot.

I tell the Giant that he will have to have a discussion with his wife. If she does not want to be seen, they can buy some painkillers from the pharmacy. I will be happy to see her, of course, but they also need to move the car. This entrance is for ambulances only. I point out an ambulance idling at the curb, awaiting access, and the other one stopped in the parking lot with the paramedic struggling to offload the stretcher on a slope.

Then I go back into the ED and pick up the first file of the day. Mr Giant and his catatonic wife will have to sort themselves out.

Half an hour later, the doorbell rings again. I see the Giant on the monitor. What is wrong with this guy? At least the car has been moved.

I walk to the triage centre and ask them to fetch the family member from the ambulance bay. He can open a file and follow the usual channels; this ringing of the ambulance access bell must stop.

I hear the Giant telling the triage nurse that he is not going to open a file because his wife does not want to see the doctor. He wants to speak to the doctor, though. It is all I can do not to snatch open the triage door and say, 'What do you want?'. Speaking to the doctor is a consultation and he should open a file. I open the triage room door with a little more zest than usual.

'I just want to ask your opinion, doctor,' the Giant tells me. I try not to fold my arms and tap my foot.

My opinion is what I give, professionally, during a meeting called a consultation.

'Yes?' I ask.

'But I can't ask you out here,' he adds, indicating the nurses and the other patients waiting to be seen.

'I am afraid if you want to consult, you will have to open a file and wait until I have seen all these people, who are ahead of you.' I indicate the packed waiting room. 'If you just want to ask me a question, I can answer it here.'

The truth is that I am prepared to answer a non-medical question if someone insists on asking me. About the weather, for instance. But if he wants to ask my opinion about something medical, I will need to get a proper history and examine the patient. And that is called a consultation.

The Giant can see that I am not going to budge on this one.

'My wife has been having these headaches for the past few months. They started after a ladder fell on her head when we were decorating for my daughter's wedding.'

'Mmmm,' I indicate for him to go on, but that is all he has to say.

'Did she have a loss of consciousness?' I ask.

'Yes,' he replies.

'How long was she unconscious for?'

'A few hours.'

'A few *hours*?' I cannot mask my surprise. 'So, has she seen a doctor? Had a scan of her brain?' I prompt.

'No.'

'Well, then, she definitely needs to consult,' I assure him.

'Can you come to the car?' he asks. 'She doesn't want to come in.'

'No, I am afraid that I cannot consult with a patient in the car in the parking lot.' I am rapidly becoming frustrated, but no 'out loud' voice I remind myself.

Eventually Mrs Giant is brought into the ED. She is tiny in stature and is soundly asleep by the time I see her. She looks like a miniature doll in comparison to her husband.

'Why is she so sleepy?' I ask the Giant. He shrugs.

A real font of information, this guy.

'So, she has had a headache for three months, after a head injury, and no other history?'

He shakes his head.

'No other symptoms?'

Getting a history from the Giant is like pulling teeth.

'Well, she says that she is dizzy. And she sleeps a lot.'

She is definitely unnaturally sleepy. When I shake her shoulder, she opens her eyes and looks at me, but falls straight back to sleep.

'Is she on any medication?' I ask. 'Painkillers?'

'No, doctor, we have no medication in our house.'

'None at all?' I ask. This seems quite strange. 'Not even paracetamol?'

'None,' he assures me.

I find the whole history bizarre. She had a head injury with a significant loss of consciousness and symptomatology afterwards and yet they have not consulted with a doctor. She locked herself in the car on arrival, and now she is barely rousable. I make a note questioning domestic violence and tick the box for drugs of overdose and a toxic screen as part of my initial investigation. I fill in a form for a brain scan.

'Can you give her something for pain?' the Giant asks.

'If she has pain, you can give me a shout and we will put something in the drip.'

I would prefer to get the blood and scan results before I give her medication, especially as she really does not appear to have any pain at all. She is fast asleep. Maybe the Giant is trying to knock her off.

When Mrs Giant comes back from x-rays, she is even more sleepy. Now she does not open her eyes at all. The blood tests and CT scan of her brain are all normal, except for the benzodiazepine level.

Benzodiazepines are sedatives and sleeping tablets. The normal blood level is less than five. Her level is 2725.

How is that even compatible with life?

She is, not surprisingly, still asleep. I find the Giant in the waiting room and show him the blood result. He looks completely blank.

'We have no sleeping tablets in our house,' he insists.

'Yep, well, that's because your wife drank them all already,' I answer in my head.

I give Mrs Giant a dose of Flumazenil, which reverses benzodiazepines. She opens her eyes five minutes later.

'Have you taken sleeping tablets?' I ask her.

She shrugs. I sigh. With such a high level, she is going to need admission to ICU. The Flumazenil will wear off before the sleeping tablets do, and she will need monitoring.

Deep sedation can easily slip over into respiratory depression.

Of course, when I do the paperwork for the admission, the clerk comes in to tell me that the Giant has not paid his medical aid because he was retrenched during lockdown. And the Giants don't have any cash at all, not even for the ED visit. Perhaps that is why they wanted to consult in the car; they figured that the clerk is unlikely to carry the credit card machine into the parking lot.

I have already arranged the admission with the physician and booked the bed in ICU. Now I must cancel all that and start calling around for a bed in a government hospital.

I'll never find out what happened wth Mr and Mrs Giant, but, like so many others, their story stays with me long after they have left.

Twelve

'Do you remember me, doctor?' a young patient looks at me expectantly over his mask.

'Um, no, sorry I actually don't,' I answer honestly. 'Have I seen you before?'

'Yes, you saved my father's life last year,' he tells me.

'Oh. That was … nice of me,' I say, relieved that there was a positive outcome.

'And you also saw me before that. I had a fondue fork stuck in my hand.'-

Now that consultation, I do recall. 'Oh yes. You used to be a Goth?'

He was part of a clan of pale young people with matt black hair and loads of piercings. The fondue fork had a barb on the back to prevent the morsels from slipping off into the communal pot. Somehow the fork had impaled his hand, right through the palm and tenting the skin on the back. Like a fishhook, once the tissue is snared on the barb, it is almost impossible to reverse. One can cut the back off and advance the sharp end of the hook forward, but a fondue fork is too thick to cut with a plier in the ED.

Yes, I remember it all very well. I think that there had been significant alcohol ingestion and there was a lot of screaming and swearing and bloodshed in the parking lot as the fellow goths tried to prize the fork out. Eventually they gave up and brought him in.

Then there was more shouting and bloodshed.

I look to see if the fondue fork has left a scar. Nothing. Seems like Goths heal well after all.

Luckily today's consultation is just an ear infection, and I can dispatch him with a script.

One of the most frustrating things about working in the ED is that I seldom get to find out what happened next for individual patients. I move on to the next crisis and rarely follow up once a patient is resuscitated and referred to a specialist. There are some families, however, that I have come to know and it is rewarding to see them flourish over the years; good to see their wounds heal and their lives move on.

I am working with a very junior doctor today. He asks me about every patient that he sees and prefaces each enquiry with 'tell me…'. He follows me around and I see about ten patients to his one. He even comes with me to the tearoom, as if he is afraid to be left alone in the ED. Which he probably is, and certainly should be. I try to be kind to him; first shifts in any new job are very anxiety provoking.

'Tell me what you think of this x-ray, Doc,' he asks sincerely. I wonder if he calls me Doc because he cannot remember my name. Truth be told, I cannot remember his. I scoot my chair over to the computer and look at the x-ray.

He reminds me of a llama, with a wild mass of curly hair and long eyelashes. He looks ready to bolt at the first sign of trouble. He picks up the red phone on the first ring and listens for a few seconds. Then he tells the caller to hang on, he is not the right person for them to speak to. He thrusts the phone at me.

'ED, Dr Anne,' I say, a bit annoyed because the Llama is also a doctor and he picked up the call, so I feel that he should at least attempt to resolve the query.

The Llama watches in amazement as I ask two questions and then tell the caller 'OK, that's fine, send 'em in.' I give my name and contact details and hang up.

'Tell me, Doc, did you just accept a patient?'

'Yep,' I say, making a note in case the patient arrives after the end of my shift.

'Just like that?'

I look up at him and waggle my eyebrows.

'Well, yes. We have beds and we have the right specialist on call, so it's OK.'

'You just took them?'

I know that, in the government hospital from whence the Llama hails, accepting a patient is a most heinous crime. I smile under my mask. 'Why make it a protracted business? If the patient is headed this way, we might as well get it over with.'

I can see him mulling this over. He trots off to see the next patient. He is back in the room within a few minutes.

'Tell me, Doc, should I drain this abscess?' I must swing by and see the patient, because I cannot give him my opinion without seeing and touching the abscess first.

'Tell me, what is the best medication to give for nappy rash?'

It goes on and on. I decide to take revenge and put an arterial blood gas result on the desk in front of him.

'Tell me, what do you think of this result?' I ask. He looks at the paper and then meets my eyes. There is a look of abject horror on his face.

'Umm, it's a blood gas,' he falters, 'what would you like to know?'

'Well, anything that you can tell me about it?'

'Don't you know?' he stammers.

'No, I can interpret the blood gas,' I say with a smile. 'But I want to see if you can. If you struggle with them, I can show you a few tricks.'

He is grateful for the help. I wish that someone had shown me how to interpret a blood gas result when I was fresh out of medical school, instead of leaving me to flounder about.

Soon he is prowling the corridor, looking for new patients. He finds one and comes straight to me. 'Doc,' he says, 'I have this patient with an ear…'

'As opposed to all the other patients in the ED, who don't have ears…' I interject. This stops him in his tracks, and he loses his train of thought completely. We stare at each other in silence.

'The patient with the ear?' I prompt him. He looks vacant for another few moments, but then finds his place.

'Tell me, how shall I get wax out of his ear?'

Suppressing a sigh, I get up to show him.

I must break the news to him that my shift is finished and that there is a two-hour gap before the next doctor comes in. He will be alone for that time. He looks completely stricken but I give him my mobile number and tell him that he can call for advice at any time. This seems to mollify him.

I go to change and have pulled my scrubs off when he opens the changing room door.

'Tell me,' he starts out and I halt, one foot in my streetwear clothes. There is a moment's hesitation and then he says '… your deepest desires.'

We both crack up laughing. The inappropriatness of the situation is immediately difused by our hysterical laughter.

Actually, I am speechless. He is young enough to be my son and I'm sure that he had no intention to say those words; he just blurted them out. He blushes deeply saying, 'Sorry, sorry. Just joking,' and pulls the door shut. I consider my options for a moment and decide not to mention the interaction further.

I think a strange intimacy can develop when two people face a stressful situation together. I have become like a mother to him over the past few hours and, unconsciously, he has formed a transference with me.

Hard to believe, I know, but it happens.

Thirteen

31 October 2020

The ED is busy but there is a momentary lull. I am heading to the kitchen with my teacup when the double doors burst open. A young paramedic backs in, towing a stretcher.

'I have a P1 patient here,' he calls over his shoulder.

No red phone, no call ahead to inform us. Charming. I put down my empty cup and eyeball the patient in the entrance corridor. He is lying on his side, arms hanging limp off the edges of the stretcher. He is completely still and ash grey in colour.

'This man is not breathing,' I tell the paramedic.

'He was breathing fine in the ambulance,' the paramedic answers defensively.

'Well, he's not breathing now,' I tell him as I flurry the stretcher into the resuscitation room. 'Move him across,' I instruct, putting my fingers on the patient's neck.

'No pulse,' I say and glance expectantly at the paramedic. I am at the airway so he should start chest compressions. Instead of putting his hands on the chest, he puts his fingers to the neck on the other side and tells me, 'There is a pulse.'

If there is a pulse, it is so weak that it does not count. And if there is any doubt, we start compressions. I check again; a faint pulse can be difficult to feel. 'No pulse,' I repeat, getting the ventilation bag off the wall hook and connecting the oxygen. I give two breaths and the sister starts compressions. The paramedic obviously has his own agenda; is he second-guessing me, I wonder. Perhaps it is a teenage testosterone surge; he looks barely fourteen years of age.

We do CPR for two minutes while a nurse gets intravenous access. The monitor shows a flat line so no shock needed; we give an ampule of adrenaline. At the rhythm check, there is a tracing on the monitor. I check the neck and now there is a pulse, but the patient is still unresponsive. I ask for a laryngoscope and tube. It is an easy intubation, and I can see the vocal cords clearly, two white wings in the dark. I aim between them and secure the tube by inflating the balloon near its tip. I take the ventilation bag off the mask and put it on the tube. A few good puffs and I look hopefully at the oxygen saturation.

The level remains below thirty per cent.

'The history here?' I ask the paramedic.

'He fell at home and hit his head. He was unconscious in the ambulance, but he woke up when we gave him oxygen.'

'So, we are thinking of a head injury?' I ask the paramedic. He shrugs and says 'Maybe'.

We are not loving each other, this teenage paramedic and me.

I ask him to get more history from the family. If the patient's heart stopped because he was not breathing well after hitting his head, his saturation should recover once we ventilate him. There must be something else wrong with him.

I switch over from the manual bag to the ventilator. I want some feedback about the pressures and airflow in the lungs. The ventilator says everything is good. Pressures are not high, good flows of oxygen. I listen to his chest for the third time. Air is moving well, and it is equal on both sides. I have another look down his throat to check my tube. There it is, snaking through the vocal cords. I can see the inflatable cuff just beyond the larynx. The tube is definitely in the right place, and it is not too deep. I suction it out in case there is a mucus plug blocking airflow. But the airway pressures are normal, and they would go up if the tube were blocked.

The saturation level is now seventeen per cent. It is going down, despite all my efforts. The pulse, not surprisingly, is faltering. No heart muscle can work with such a poor oxygen supply. This patient is dying in front of me, and it seems that there is not much I can do to change the trajectory.

'The saturations are low,' the paramedic tells me.

I wonder if he thinks I am a complete idiot. I bite back a sharp retort and ask him if he has found out more about the history. It turns out that there was no fall and no head injury. The patient felt faint and breathless at home and his grandson helped him to a chair. He subsequently lost consciousness. So, we are looking at a medical reason, rather than trauma-related cause, for his cardiac and respiratory arrest.

The saturation is now ten per cent and the patient's heart stops again. My heart sinks as I put my hands on his chest and start compressions. Grim has got the better of me here. The only thing that I can think of which would cause such poor oxygen saturation in a patient with a normal chest x-ray, good airflow and normal lung compliance is a clot in the lungs. Called a pulmonary embolism, the clot prevents blood getting to the alveoli to fetch oxygen. So, the air is moving, bringing plenty of oxygen in, but the blood is not able to get to the pick-up point, absorb it and take it to the body.

Once the heart has already stopped, there is not much that I can do about a massive pulmonary embolism. Maybe some heroics like intravenous blood thinners, but I haven't had much luck with them in cases like this.

The general surgeon pops her head around the door. She has come to see another patient in the ED. 'Need any help?' she asks sweetly.

'Well, if you can figure out why this man's oxygen saturation is so low, that would help me,' I reply.

My own haemoglobin is still low, and the effort of chest compressions is making me breathless.

She correctly takes this as an invitation to join the resuscitation and steps into the room. We have a pulse back, thanks to the adrenaline in the drip.

The surgeon goes through all the same steps. She investigates the airway with the laryngoscope. Disconnects, examines and reconnects the tubing. Checks the ventilator and the capnograph, which monitors carbon dioxide levels. Listens to the chest, looks at the chest x-ray and glances at the blood gas print out.

'It's a massive pulmonary embolism,' she concludes.

To make herself useful, she puts up a central line for better intravenous access. We both know that this resuscitation is going nowhere, but we have a pulse back now and so we must press on.

The paramedic comes around the bed and adjusts the ventilator settings. The surgeon, who does not tolerate fools gladly, tells him not to touch the ventilator.

'The patient needs increased PEEP,' the paramedic tells her scornfully. The letters stand for positive end expiratory pressure and mean that the ventilator leaves a bit of air in the lungs at the end of the exhalation, helping to hold the lung tissues open.

'There is nothing wrong with the PEEP setting,' she says quickly, her tone matching his. 'Put it back to five.'

The paramedic looks chastened and slinks away.

'How old is that guy anyway?' she mumbles under her breath, as she glides a guidewire into her central line. I smile to myself. She reminds me of the Professor, who reigned with an iron fist when women surgeons were unheard of and blazed a trail for those who followed.

The saturations drop to seven per cent and the patient flat lines again. I shake my head and call an end to the resuscitation efforts. Before everyone walks away, I ask for a moment to respect the life that has passed and give thought to the family in this time. The teenage paramedic stares at me as if I have grown a horn in the middle of my forehead.

I pull the sheet up over the patient's face and go in search of the family.

The patient was elderly, and the family accepts the news with calm equanimity. This makes my job so much easier and is unusual with an unexpected death.

The paediatric surgeon is waiting for me in the doctors, room. I called him to see a little boy with appendicitis and he is awaiting an introduction. I think it was very kind of him to wait for me to finish with resuscitation and the bereaved family, and I take him through to meet his patient.

The child looks well in himself, playing on his father's mobile and asking for juice. I have told them not to let him eat or drink anything until they see the specialist.

Understandably, the family has a heap of questions, and the surgeon spends a good half an hour with them before booking the little boy for theatre. He is only two, and the sonar confirms that his appendix has already burst. Young children usually don't give us much warning, and there is a low index of suspicion as appendicitis is very unusual in this age group.

I look longingly at my empty teacup, but the lull has passed, and we are back at full tilt. Mercifully, the hours are flying by, and things are going relatively smoothly until I hear the shrill beep of the emergency pager. The sister retrieves it from the nursing station desk, checks the screen and calls 'Resuscitation in the paediatric ward!'

We grab the resuscitation bag and dash along the corridor. It has been many years since I have been called to assist in the paediatric ward and I feel anxious. No one likes paediatric resuscitations.

It does not occur to me that the child who has arrested is the little boy who had his appendix out. It is only when I recognise the shell-shocked parents standing outside the room and the horribly still body of the two-year-old boy on the bed that I connect the dots.

'Oh no,' I think to myself. 'This is not good. Not good at all.'

The team kicks into action. CPR, intubate, basic bloods, chest x-ray. The paediatrician and surgeon arrive hot on my heels and there are more than enough hands.

But all the hands in the world are not bringing this little boy back to life.

We call the resuscitation off after about an hour of trying. The surgeon and I lock eyes for a moment. I have some idea of how big a deal this is going to be; how today will change the course of his life.

'The surgery was uneventful. He woke up well in recovery and was a little restless for a few hours but settled in the ward.' I can see that he is going over and over the case in his head, trying to figure out what went wrong. 'I hope I don't get assassinated in the car park,' he adds, under his breath. I want to hug him, but it would be inappropriate in front of the grieving family. The mum rocks backwards and forwards, unseeing, while the dad weeps uncontrollably.

The surgeon and paediatrician are trying to counsel them. I pack my equipment and slither away. There is nothing further for me to do here.

Towards the end of the day, I finally get to make my cup of tea. The paediatric surgeon is in the theatre tearoom, and he looks shattered.

'Kill anyone else?' he asks.

'Not today,' I say ruefully. 'I'm trying to cut down. You?'

'One's enough.'

We share a moment of silence and understanding. We will press on, because there will be more battles with Grim, and maybe some that we can win. Today will never be forgotten, but it will be replaced by tomorrow's challenges.

Fourteen

9 November 2020

The sister asks me to take a call on the red phone and I ask who is calling. This pedantic habit has evolved after years of fending off insurance brokers and investment consultants, who call the switchboard and ask for the doctor on call. Patients also sometimes use the emergency number to ask for advice.

If I have seen the patient previously, I am very happy to consult on the telephone. People often have questions about the medication prescribed or the follow-up plan. But I cannot advise a person that I have never met with a problem that I did not diagnose. I certainly cannot telephonically change the plan of action or medication given by another doctor who has physically seen the patient. For all these cases, my advice remains the same.

I tell them that they need to come into the ED.

I feel that this simple sentence can be said effectively by any person who answers the phone. It is quite easy to understand. I have even written it out as a flow chart, laminated it, and pasted it next to the red phone. But the call hardly ever goes as planned.

'Is that the ED?'

'Yes, it is. How may I help you?'

'I want to speak to the doctor.'

'May I ask who is calling?'

Now the flow chart divides.

Possibility one: 'I am calling from an insurance or investment company.'

Response: 'The doctors are all very busy at present. I can take your number and they will call back if they are interested.'

Possibility two: 'It is Doctor X. I need to refer a patient.'

Response: 'Please hold on, I will call her.'

Possibility three: 'It is Mrs Z. I need to ask for advice.'

Response: 'Have you seen the doctor before?'

'Yes, but I am not sure of something.'

'Please hold on, I will find your file and call the doctor. If she is busy with an emergency, I can take your number and she will call you back.'

If the caller has not seen the doctor before, here comes the difficult line.

'If you have not seen the doctor before, the best way forward is to come into the ED and consult. There are some practices that offer telephonic consultations under specific circumstances, but this ED does not offer that service.'

It amazes me that more than half the patients cannot, or will not, understand this. I see the sisters holding the phone away from their ear while the caller yells at them. Today, the nurse is at the end of her tether.

'Please take this call, doctor.' She sounds so desperate that, against my better judgement, I take the handset from her.

'Hello?' I say.

'Is that the doctor?' A grumpy-sounding man asks.

'Yes, it is. Doctor Anne.'

'What is your surname?' he asks snappily.

I grind my teeth. 'Biccard.'

'Spell it, he commands.

'It is spelled exactly as it is said. And your name?' I can hear a slight snippiness in my tone.

He does not want to tell me his name. Perhaps he thinks that I am going to send him a bill.

'I have this rash on my legs. I went to my general practitioner, and he gave me medication, but it is not helping.'

'What is the name of the medication that you got?'

'I don't know. It didn't work so I threw it away.'

With rashes, it is important to know what medication did not work, as well as the ones that did. This information helps to make a diagnosis.

'It was a small white tablet. Useless,' he adds, testily. I tell him that there are hundreds of small white tablets on the market and that I cannot diagnose a rash over the phone.

I tell him that he needs to come into the ED.

'And get Covid?' His tone is incredulous. 'And pay another consultation just to get more useless advice from the medical profession?'

No out-loud voice, I remind myself.

'Could you hold the phone a little closer to the rash so that I can see it better?' I ask.

The dial tone blares in my ear as he hangs up. I shake my head. A few seconds later the red phone trills again. I pick it up on the first ring; I am ready for him this time.

'ED. Dr Anne speaking.'

'Is that the doctor?' a tremulous voice asks.

'Yes, it is.' I am feeling curt.

'I wonder if you can help me,' she stifles a sob, 'I think my cat is dead. But I am not sure. How can I tell?'

'Umm, well, where is the cat now?'

'He is under the cupboard. But he has been there for a few days, not moving, and he is very old.'

'You are going to have to pull him out,' I tell her.

'How?' I can hear the uncertainty in her voice.

'Just take the leg nearest to you and pull gently. I will wait on the line.'

I hear her scuffling about and a few more muted sobs. 'OK, he's out. He is just lying here. Maybe he's sleeping.'

'Are his ribs moving at all?' I ask. 'Is he breathing?'

I feel like a 911 dispatcher.

'No.'

'Are his eyes open or closed?'

'Open.'

'I don't think he is sleeping then. Take a little piece of tissue paper and touch it on his eyeball. If he doesn't blink, and he is not breathing, then he is dead.'

More scuffling and sobs and she returns with the news that he is dead.

'What shall I do now, doctor? Do I need to get a death certificate?'

'Um, ah ... no, you can just bury him in your garden if you want to. Or the vets offer a cremation service.'

'OK. Thanks, doctor.' She sounds so grateful, and I feel sad for her as I hang up the phone. I suppose that what is obvious to me may not seem that obvious to others.

Either that, or the lady was pranking me. She sounded too sincere though, and what kind of macabre joke would that be to play? If it were a prank, I am sure that karma will catch up with her.

No sooner is the red phone back in its cradle than it rings again. I snatch it up. I think that it might be the rash guy again, but it is the senior paramedic on our team. He sounds completely stressed out. They were called out to a patient who was attacked by a swarm of bees. The gardener was mowing the lawn and the sound of the engine, or the smell of petrol, set them off. They swarmed after her into the house and now the paramedics can see the patient, unconscious on the floor, but there are too many bees to go inside.

I know that another ambulance service has bee protection suits in their response vehicle, and I ask them to assist. I have their control room number on speed dial, and they can be on scene within a few minutes.

Ten minutes later, the Bee Lady arrives in the ED. She is still fully clothed and there are bees all over her. In her mouth, her ears and her hair. She is absolutely covered in bee stings; hundreds and hundreds of them.

She looks like a trimmed prickly pear.

The paramedics have already given her injections of adrenaline and antihistamines through the fabric of her dress. She is conscious and able to talk but we are going to run into trouble here. I call the physician and ask him to be on standby for a difficult airway. We get her clothing off and pick off the remaining bees. There is one in her ear that I cannot reach, and I ask the ENT to come down to the ED and help. I also want him to look at her airway to assess if there is swelling further down than I can see. Her tongue and lips are mildly swollen, and she is not wheezing, but the paramedics have given medication that could disguise these signs.

The physician and the ENT arrive in the resuscitation room at the same time. They are friends and banter with each other as the ENT sets up his camera and feeds it through the Bee Lady's nose. The airway does not look too bad, but I still think that we need to intubate her. It is much easier to put the tube in now, when there are three doctors and three nurses right at the bedside, and a very nice video view of where you are trying to go. The alternative is to wait and see; but then, if the airway swells shut, there is no way we will get a tube down. We would have to resort to a surgical airway, which means making a hole in the windpipe. And chances are that we will lose the airway in the middle of the night, with some lone junior doctor attempting a procedure that she has never done before. Despite tales of fellow diners plunging a steak knife into a choking victim's neck, it is not the easiest thing to do.

Especially not when the patient is suffocating in front of you.

Both the physician and the ENT agree with me, and we explain everything to the Bee Lady. As I am about to give sedation, I check with her again if she is allergic to anything. This is an ingrained habit that I ask before I put pen to paper for a prescription or press the plunger to give medication.

'Bees,' she says, and rolls her eyes. Luckily, she is not allergic to bees, as she would be long dead by now. But I am sure she will welcome the oblivion of sedation; what a nightmare the last half an hour must have been for her.

The intubation goes smoothly with the physician doing the airway while the ENT keeps an eye with video laryngoscopy and swirls oil into the Bee Lady's ear to retrieve two bees.

Bee Lady is packaged off to ICU and I am slightly optimistic about her chances of survival.

The physician comes down to ED later in the day and tells me that he has started inotropes on the Bee Lady. This is not a good sign. Inotropes are drugs that increase the strength of the heart muscle contraction and are used when the blood pressure drops, and the organs are not being perfused. Once a patient, like the Bee Lady, needs inotropes, Grim has clocked his presence and is making his inexorable way towards her bedside.

Sure enough, when I walk up to ICU the next morning, I find an empty bed where Bee Lady was. Cot sides up and a naked mattress, wiped clean. My heart is heavy for her family, who looked at me with such hope when I met with them yesterday. I suppose that it was just too much venom for her body to deal with.

I am a great champion of the bee and am always on the lookout for ways to assist them, but any humming noise makes me overwhelmingly anxious for a good few weeks to come.

Fifteen

20 November 2020

It sounds like there are renovations happening in the ED. There is relentless hammering, but I can also hear shouting as I make my way in through the double doors. It is slightly muffled, but a man is calling out someone's name. I set my bag and lunch container down in the doctors room and go in search of the origin of the commotion.

There is not another person in sight, but I find an elderly man lying alone in a cubicle at the end of the corridor. The bed rails are up, and he is hammering on the wall with his walking stick. He is shouting 'Sarie' repeatedly.

Bang, bang, bang. 'Sarie. Sarie. Saaaarrriee!'

I go to him and ask what he needs. He glances at me briefly and then resumes his chant. 'SarEEEEE,' he yells. I take the walking stick away from him and there is a welcome silence for a few moments. No sooner have I walked back to the doctors room to find out about the patient from the night doctor than the banging starts again. This time he is hitting the drywalling with his fist. 'Sarie!' he yells. I go back into the room and take the brake off the bed. I roll the bed into the centre of the room and clip the brake on again.

The patient glares balefully at me through the cot side railings.

'You can't keep me here,' he tells me. 'I am a free citizen.'

'Okay,' I say agreeably.

'Where is Sarie? I am thirsty.'

'I'm not sure where Sarie is,' I answer, 'but I can get you some water.'

'I'm cold,' he adds. I fetch a blanket and a cup of water.

'I'm tired,' he tells me when I get back.

'Have a nap then. I will switch off the light.' I flip the switch at the door, and he tells me again that he is a free citizen. Within moments of my departure, he starts shouting for help. It is distressing but he does not seem to be in pain.

'Help! Help me! SarEEEE!'

What a way to start my shift. I wonder where all the staff has gone and what the story with the elderly man is. When the night doctor eventually emerges, he tells me that the man is already admitted and is waiting for a bed.

The Covid numbers are climbing again. We have gone for a few weeks with no cases admitted. Yesterday, there were two. Today, there are four. Same kind of presentation, same looking chest x-ray.

I'm not sure that I have it in me to go through this all again.

We have become complacent. Patients with coughs and fever stand right next to other patients in the waiting room.

This resurgence has a slightly different flavour when compared to the first wave. People seem sicker and there are many more of them. But the containers have been removed, and we are back to one emergency room with a few cubicles and resuscitations bays.

Keeping Covid from spreading feels like allocating a place for a person to urinate in a crowded pool.

I keep reminding people to keep their masks on. This is almost impossible in young children who just rip it away, shred it with their teeth or wipe it off on the nearest adult.

We are all tired and fed up with everything. But I also have a creeping sense that there is more to this virus than meets the eye. It makes no sense to me. There is a complete disconnect between what I find when I examine the patient and what I see on the investigations. Usually pneumonia can be heard, with faint or coarse crackles as the wet lung inflates, and changes in the sound of the air flow. The lungs of patients with Covid pneumonia sound perfect. No wheezing, no crackles.

But the chest x-ray slaps you in the face with the most shocking changes and the blood results are off the charts.

It feels like I am in the middle of a hurricane, but I cannot feel the wind on my skin. There is something very sinister about it all.

I am considering the strangeness of this virus when I hear the unit manager calling my name. I pop my head out of the office.

'I'm here,' I call.

I see her moving away from me down the corridor, and my mobile rings. It is she, phoning now; there must be a problem.

'I'm here,' I say again. 'What's wrong?'

I can only hear rustling and cracking. Maybe it is a pocket dial. I pursue her down the corridor and catch up with her in the last cubicle. There is a young lady on the bed, holding a blood-soaked towel to her nose. In her other hand, she is holding an ice cream container. Last time I checked, those containers hold two litres of ice cream. It is at least half-full of blood. The unit manager spots me and beckons me closer.

'This lady has a bad nosebleed,' she tells me.

You can say that again, I think. It is like a fire hydrant, pouring through the towel and into the container.

I send the unit manager to get a special nose pack and wonder if blood is heavier than ice cream. I think it should be, with all that iron in it. Either way, she has lost at least a litre of blood.

Introducing myself, I smear antibiotic cream all over the nose plug and push it into her nostril. I inflate the plug with air, then wipe her face and chest.

The smell of clotting blood is strong and specific It always reminds me of the intake pit at Baragwanath Hospital. If I close my eyes, I am right back there.

'Sorry to have assaulted you with the nose plug, but we needed to get that blood under control,' I tell her.

I use a tongue depressor to check there is no bleeding running down the back of her throat. 'It looks like it has stopped. How do you feel?'

She is pale and she tells me that she is thirsty and dizzy. The unit manager has gone to get the equipment for an intravenous line and, in the meantime, I tilt the bed back so that the patient is lying flat. Just in time, because she passes out and the blood pressure monitor alarms repeatedly.

We are quick with the drip, and I open the wheel to let the whole litre run in. It takes a few minutes until we can get a blood pressure reading and her colour looks a bit better.

I keep her in the unit for observation for a few hours. Her haemoglobin is stable and she feels better. The nose plug is doing its job and there is no more bleeding. I decide to let her go home and we will recheck her haemoglobin in the morning when she comes to get the nose plug out. She has lost a lot of blood, but we are reluctant to transfuse patients who are otherwise well and stable. I give her a script for an iron supplement and write down my name so that she can find me easily on her return.

That was a close call. I have never seen a nose bleeding that vigorously. Perhaps I need to lace my tea with valium, to make me feel as calm as I pretend to be.

Sixteen

10 December 2020

The second wave of the corona infection has been formally declared. A surge over the weekend, mostly in young people who attended super spreader events, has pushed the country back into crisis.

Super spreader is a term for a person who, once infected, seems to shed the virus more heavily, resulting in many more of their contacts being infected than would normally be the case. In viral pandemics, it seems that one in five people may be super spreaders. Put this individual in a crowd where there is poor airflow, absence of social distancing and no PPE, and the result is a super spreader event.

Like ripples on a pond, we are dealing with the fallout from these events, many of which were post-matric festivities. I am wondering how organisers got permission to hold them, and why parents allowed their children to attend, given the fact that we are mirroring the rest of the world, with a three-month lag time.

I am just tired of it all.

My next patient tells me that she has a lizard in her ear. She saw it go in.

There are several inconsistencies with this story. How would she see a lizard shimmying into her ear, unless she was looking in the mirror? And, if she were watching it, why didn't she stop it? I cannot think of any urban lizards native to Johannesburg that would fit into the average ear.

Nevertheless, she has opened a file and been brought through as a priority two patient, so I look in her ear with the otoscope.

Not surprisingly, there is nothing in her ear at all. No wax. No insects. Certainly, no reptiles.

The problem is that she doesn't believe me.

'Are you sure?' she asks repeatedly. 'Check again.' She flicks her hair back and tilts her head obligingly. 'I saw it go in.'

'Well, it is not in there now,' I reassure her. I can see that she is dissatisfied with the consultation but what can I do? I wonder briefly if they sell toy lizards at the coffee shop and if I could somehow conceal it in my sleeve and miraculously present it.

I immediately reprimand myself for this line of thinking. Deception will not do.

ENTs have a video system so that the patient can see what they are looking at with the otoscope, but we don't have that fancy equipment in the ED. I am the only one who can see in there and she is going to have to just take my word for it.

After all, why would I lie.

We part ways with a vague sense of dissatisfaction, which I perceive as mutual.

During the lizard consultation, I can hear the phone in the doctors' room ringing incessantly. It is a lonely sound, a single phone trilling in a deserted area. Calling out rhythmically, with no one to pick it up. Eventually I get to answer it. I feel like being under cover, so I just say, 'Hello?'

'Hello. Is that the doctor?'

'Yes?'

'Ah, good, it is Mary from the theatre complex. Dr Anderson asked me to call the ED and ask if you have Dr Nel's cellular number.'

'I do,' I reply, 'but Dr Nel is working with Dr Anderson today.'

I know them both well and have worked out the pattern of their theatre lists. 'They will be in theatre three.'

'I am in theatre three with Dr Anderson,' Mary tells me. 'We need to get hold of Dr Nel urgently.'

I look at the clock – it is after five in the evening – and wonder why these two doctors are doing such a long list. They are both around eighty years of age and, although they are still competent, they should be thinking of retiring.

I look up Dr Nel's number on my mobile and read it to Mary. I make a cup of tea and settle down to write a few notes, but the call is bothering me.

Maybe Dr Anderson has a complication or a case that needs to go back to theatre. We have worked together for years, and we have become friends. If he has a problem, I feel that I should help him. He is a hot-tempered Scotsman but has a heart of gold.

Not much is happening in the ED, so I get changed into clean scrubs, put a theatre hat and some shoe covers on and nip through the back door to the operating complex.

Theatre three is the only one in use and the overhead lights are bright behind the swing doors. Through the porthole window I see a patient on the table, fully draped, and Dr Anderson sitting on a stool, staring at the monitors. I rap on the glass, and he turns to face me. I wave and he beckons me in.

'What's happening?' I ask. Everything looks under control to me. Anderson is grey now, but he was a flaming redhead in his youth, and he has not lost his Scottish brogue.

'My anaesthetist has not shown up. Mary saw him earlier but now he's done a runner. She has gone to give him a bell. There's no reception down here.'

Mary bumps open the door from the scrub room.

'He's at the supermarket!' she announces. 'He put the patient under anaesthetic and then went to the changeroom to take a pee while I cleaned and draped. But he saw his clothes hanging there, he had a brief lapse, and forgot that the patient was still on the table and that we were starting, not finished. He dressed and went to do some late shopping.'

She takes a deep breath, and says, 'He is on his way back.'

I can see that Dr Anderson is amazed, although does not say a word.

I am reminded of another doctor, a gynaecologist, who was way past his sell-by date. He was examining a lady in a side ward when he got called to an emergency. In all the excitement, he totally forgot about the side ward lady and went home once the emergency was resolved. A few hours later I happened down that corridor to hear a plaintive, 'Help…'. When I opened the door, there was this lady, lying with her feet in the stirrups and a speculum in place.

I make a mental note that I must put myself out to pasture whilst I can still find my way home.

Seventeen

21 December 2020

To celebrate the summer solstice, Coro Coro is back with a vengeance. The wards are full, and things are definitely much worse than the first time around. On top of which we are hopelessly short-staffed and honestly exhausted.

Some staff have taken leave despite the skyrocketing figures and, today, we are down to less than half of our usual team. Sick leave and end-of-year leave have decimated the ranks and there is also a spike in young doctors taking ED jobs overseas.

I find it strange that they are emigrating during a pandemic. I am sure that they pay well, and many South Africans have been waiting for an opportunity to make a change, but why would one expose oneself to another whole wave and strain of the coronavirus? In a country full of strangers and unknown resources?

I think it is much worse to die on foreign soil and my mind goes briefly to all the young men who died in far-flung wars.

We are an oddity, the human race.

The thought of being trapped in an aeroplane for nine hours with recirculated air and hundreds of fellow travellers practically sitting on your lap gives *me* the shivers, and I am seeing twenty or thirty positive coronavirus patients per day.

Those doctors must really, really want to leave.

The team is ratty and tired. For the first time in my life, the unit manager snaps at me and doesn't even smile at my jokes. I am making bat wings with my plastic gown, speeding around the unit with my arms outstretched, and she tells me to stop fooling around. It is impossible for her to manage the unit, with all the administration involved, as well as look after sick patients. I can see that she is exhausted, so I stop my antics and order pizza for the team. Amazing, the health benefits of a five-minute break and a slice of warm pizza.

Last night the WhatsApp groups had a flurry of messages reminding us that the ED is not allowed to turn patients away. People must be seen, regardless of resources and bed availability. Someone in management tells us that we are not a burger franchise, which closes when they run out of burgers.

I am aware of that. But, at some point, we will run out of burgers. We will keep the lights on, keep showing up for work, but once the last patty and bun is gone, there will be no more.

People are complaining about the beaches being closed. I want to shake them and remind them that, if all their loved ones get sick at the same time, we will not be able to help them. Surely this stands to reason. I would love to go to the beach, but right now is not a good time.

It feels like South Africa, and the world at large, are skating on very thin ice.

My phone starts to vibrate again. The next slew of messages is to remind us that we are only allowed one N95 mask per shift and we must not put them down on the tables or desks as they are contaminated and will spread corona. I wonder what we are supposed to do with them between patients. Hang them on our ear, perhaps, or just continue to wear them for ten hours at a stretch.

The constant fear of the virus, for our patients and ourselves, is exhausting. But so is the not knowing. The perpetual debate and uncertainty, the ebb and the flow; it is like being at war.

I am back to being suspicious of my shoes and lining them up on the patio wall. I am sure that they are teeming with germs. I fear that I may be developing a hand-washing fetish. The snoopies wait while I disembark from the car and take my shoes off. They are like shiny, silent shadows, ever watchful. And then, one by one they bound up, touching me with their giant noses and running huge loops of delight on the lawn.

Pookie has a broken leg and is in a plaster cast. He cannot make it over the uneven terrain to the farm gate. He waits on the patio, his green eyes shining and his little caramel body squirming in delight.

'Roooo,' he tilts his square nose to the sky. 'Rooooo. Roooo!'

He has become too heavy to pick up, so I bend to smooth his velvet face. His skin is so fine and soft, I wonder how he was bred to fight.

I look into his smiling eyes and wish all the horribleness in the world would just go away.

Eighteen

23 December 2020

The container is back outside the hospital but this time it is for screening people who want to travel internationally. They need a negative corona test within forty-eight hours of their flight. At six in the morning, the queue of people waiting to be screened coils through the parking lot.

I want to ask them all what they are thinking. Elective travel during a pandemic seems out of touch and, frankly, deluded.

Some people are worried about being tagged and electronically monitored by a microchip in the vaccination. These may be the same people who use GPS in their cars and on their phones; tag themselves and others on social media, count their steps and workouts with tracking devices and enter their details on every electronic platform available.

Now they are worried that they will be tracked by an injectable microchip and that the vaccine is actually the evil brainchild of the lizards who run the world.

I have some concerns about the vaccination, but electronic tracking is not one of them.

The triage sister trots through the double doors, pushing a wheelchair. The lady slouched therein is weeping in pain. All the beds are full, so she travels the length of the unit until she reaches the only vacant one. She halts the wheelchair at the foot of the empty bed, expecting the patient to get up and move over. Nothing, aside from the wailing, is happening. I am working in the next cubicle, and I pull the curtain aside. I look down at the patient's feet and see that her right foot is facing backwards at the ankle. The sister follows my line of sight and, without expression, turns the wheelchair around and takes it to the resuscitation room.

We will need to sedate her to put the ankle back in place; and time is of the essence. The displaced bone is causing pressure on the surrounding tissue and pushing the blood flow away, which can result in infection, disability and even amputation.

When I was newly qualified, I called the orthopod for a case exactly like this. He told me that he never wanted to see an x-ray of a displaced broken ankle. 'Always,' he told me sternly, 'reduce the dislocation as soon as you can sedate the patient. Don't waste time sending the patient to x-rays. The ankle is clearly broken and dislocated. Restoring the correct anatomy is of the utmost urgency.'

I took his advice to heart and have repeated it to many others over the years.

I give the weeping lady some anaesthetic gas while we get ready to sedate her. She is crying too much to make good use of the inhalant, which works best if you take long pulls and hold it in your lungs. She is thrashing around, her foot flopping backwards and sideways with each movement. She keeps taking the mask off her face.

'It's so sore! It's so sore! Don't put it on the bed,' she howls, but the alternative is to hold her lower leg up in the air, which leaves the foot dangling at an even more alarming angle.

In record time, we get her attached to all the monitors, have the drip up and get our hands on a vial of propofol from the locked drug cupboard. We have our resuscitation equipment in place in case we go too far.

Her head shoots up as I draw up the propofol. It is a murky white liquid, and some anaesthetists call it the milk of amnesia.

'Is that morphine?' she asks.

'No,' I reply. 'It's better than morphine.'

'I want morphine,' her head sinks back. 'Please give me morphine.'

'Mmmmm, well this is good stuff. It will make you sleep,' I tell her as I connect the syringe to the port in her intravenous line.

Her head shoots up again. 'It isn't working yet!'

'I haven't even given it yet,' I tell her with a slight tease in my voice. 'But here it comes.' I chase the milky stream through the tubing by opening the drip wide, and within ten seconds her eyes glaze over.

I move to the foot of the bed to do the reduction but, as I touch her skin, her eyes fly open. 'I'm not sleeping yet,' she tells me.

Huh, I think. I go back to the drip and top up the propofol. Her eyes glaze over again but by the time I am back in position at her foot, she is awake again.

She is guzzling up the drug in record time.

I have had a few patients who have gone to sleep on a lick of propofol and just don't wake up. That is why we always have a full resuscitation trolley next to the bed. Once you sleep too deeply, you stop breathing and so every sedation must have the equipment ready to breathe for the patient.

I give the syringe of propofol to the nurse and ask her to give the remaining third. The first two thirds should be well out of her system as propofol has a short half-life, which means that it gets metabolised quickly. I stay at the ankle while she gives it and, as it slithers into her vein, I pull the foot and ankle back into alignment.

It makes a satisfying crunch and I hold it up by the big toe while the sister wraps the wool and plaster cast around the ankle.

On the x-ray you can barely even see the break and you could be fooled into thinking that the cast will do the trick. But for an ankle to deform so badly, the bones are broken, and the ligaments torn. They will need to be pinned and plated. This young lady is going to be spending her festive season in a hospital bed with her leg suspended from the ceiling.

We have a new assistant in the unit. She is only starting formally in the new year, but she is here for orientation today. She seems keen and asks if she can see a few patients herself and then present them to me. I agree, despite this being tedious for me, as it is the only way to learn.

She goes to the first cubicle and I to the second. I hear her taking a laborious history from her patient, who is obfuscating. Maybe he has a sore throat, he feels a bit achy, feverish even. Listening to his history in parallel with my patient's is like trying to catch the lyrics in two songs being played at the same time.

Pretty much impossible.

I nudge the curtain back with my foot and tell the assistant to get the nurse in PPE to do a rapid Covid test on the patient before the assistant spends any more time in the cubicle.

The rapid test looks for the antigen on the virus and is quick and reliable.

One sister is designated to do rapids each day and she trawls the unit in PPE, sticking long ear buds up people's noses and then mixing the mucous swabbed with a reagent. She drips the mix on a window in a small plastic square and waits for the stripes. One stripe is negative. Two stripes are positive. No stripes mean that the test did not work.

Exactly like a pregnancy test.

While she is waiting for the fluid to sweep across the reagent strip, she chats to the patient. 'It's not really a sore throat that I came in for,' he tells her. 'It is more the pain in my arm and hand that is bothering me.'

I pull the curtain back again and look at the test. It looks like it is going to be negative.

'Which arm is painful?' I ask.

It is his left arm.

'Are you having chest pain?' I ask.

'Well, yes, a bit in my chest and neck but more in my arm.'

His beard is yellow with nicotine, and he answers my questions about risk factors with a definite yes to all.

I ask the sister to do an ECG. With his age, smoking and other risk factors, I think that the history of fever and body aches is taking us down the wrong road.

Sure enough, he is having a heart attack. A big one. We move him quickly to the resuscitation room, even though he has been having the pain since yesterday morning, and activate the cardiologist and catheterisation team. The assistant looks a bit bewildered. I try to show her the abnormalities on the ECG, but it is hard to know what is abnormal if you have no idea of what is normal.

The cardiologist on call today is one of my favourites. He is soft spoken, sincere and very knowledgeable. He comes immediately to the ED and sees the patient. We agree on the path forward. He is still busy with the echocardiogram, which is a sonar of the heart, when a lady crashes through the double doors of the ED.

'HELP!!' She screams, an unresponsive toddler in her arms. 'He drowned! He drowned! Help him, help him…' she drops to her knees, and I snatch the child from her.

'Quick, quick, let's get him on the bed and start CPR!' I call to my team. I seldom use the word 'quick', and it sets them all running. I turn back into the resuscitation room. There are no free beds but at least there is some equipment. Yellow beard jumps off his bed to make way for us. The cardiologist takes his arm and hustles him to a chair in the corridor.

I put the boy on the bed. No pulse. No breathing. Damn, damn, damn!

I grab the resuscitation bag and mask and start to do breaths.

'Do you know how to do chest compressions?' I ask the person in the corner. I thought it was the assistant, who was standing there a second ago, but it turns out that she ran to get help and the only other person in the room is the cleaner. She does not answer me either, but just backs rapidly out of the room.

In this moment, with this unresponsive, drenched little boy, I say a flash prayer to the Professor who teaches advanced life support. He runs us through drill after drill, until it all starts to fit together. He starts and ends each course with the same words: 'I want my team to run towards the emergency, not away from it.'

I am also mindful of how valuable that call on the red phone is. Even if it is from a member of the public, telling us to expect an emergency gives us a head start. We can get the bed clear, don gloves and masks and allocate roles.

There are running feet and shouting as the whole team is activated. This group has worked together for many years and the equipment materialises next to the bed like magic.

The shift leader is quickly onto the chest with compressions, and I keep squeezing the bag to try and get some air moving. We lay a tape next to the little boy to measure him and get an approximate weight. The paediatric resuscitation bag has different compartments with the right sized equipment for each weight group. They are colour coded to help us move with speed and certainty.

I dial the paediatrician on call to help me as I am the only doctor in the ED, and I need hands.

She arrives as we intubate the patient and gets busy with drawing up drugs. She knows the doses per kilogram without hesitation and adrenaline is soon squirted down the tube. She uses a little drill to get access to the bone marrow and give drugs. There is no chance of putting up an intravenous line in a chubby toddler with no blood pressure.

The adrenaline flows in. I see the cardiologist standing in the corner of the room, watching the chaos unfold. I beckon him over and ask him to put his echo probe on the little boy's chest. It is my turn to do chest compressions and I stop for five seconds to let him look.

Nothing. Not even a flutter where his little heart is. Just perfect, still anatomy.

My hands are back on the chest.

'Pump harder,' the paediatrician tells me. I am already pushing hard, but I add some vigor. Perspiration is cascading down my face.

'How long was the baby in the water?' I ask a sister to find out.

They are not sure. My heart is sinking. We have been going for almost an hour. Grim has got this one and none of us want to let go. Core temperature was thirty-one when we checked it a few minutes in. Now it is almost thirty-six. There is an old trauma unit adage that you are not dead until you are warm and dead. There is an outside chance that, when you correct the hypothermia, you may get the patient back. I have seen it once in all my years of practice; but sadly, I won't be pulling that rabbit out of this hat today. I give him another round of drugs, another fifteen minutes to be absolutely sure. Then I stop squeezing the bag.

'Guys, I'm going to call this resuscitation.'

We all stand in miserable silence. Pink froth seeps up the tube which is secured with tape. The intraosseous catheter still stands proud from his little leg. I ask the cardiologist to do one more echo.

Nothing.

'OK,' I say. 'That is the easy part of our job, done. Now comes the difficult part.'

I open the door and take a deep breath before I decimate the parents' lives. The paediatrician is the mother of a few toddlers herself. She could have just ducked out, but she stays and stands shoulder to shoulder with me.

Mom looks at us with fear and a little bit of hope. Dad knows from the look on our faces and immediately dissolves into wretched sobbing.

There are no words, but I try to find some. I put my hand on the dad's shoulder as his body heaves with grief. His mobile phone rings and he presses it silent. In that moment his screen saver comes up. It is a beautiful picture of the little boy at his birthday, a huge cake with two candles in the foreground.

His face is so happy, so shiny and hopeful; his family crowded in the back of the image, all looking at him with bright eyes.

The picture is so full of love and hope. It absolutely breaks my heart.

Nineteen

24 December 2020

Christmas Eve and we have recorded the highest number of Covid infections in South Africa over the past twenty-four hours. Since yesterday morning, 14 000 new cases have been recorded; the previous peak was 13 994 on 24 July. The second wave also seems to be spreading much faster and making people sicker. There were 411 deaths from corona over the past twenty-four hours, which is the second highest daily death rate in our history of this pandemic.

The ambulances are supposed to call ahead to tell us if they are bringing in a known Covid patient, but I think that no one is answering the landline, so they just arrive, chiming the doorbell over and over. We only have eight beds in the Covid positive section, and, at present, all those beds are full.

The doorbell alternates tunes, but at present it is stuck on the theme song from *The Titanic*. It is both fitting and annoying.

The paramedics have a new lime green look and stand outside the door in their dayglo space suits, a stretcher in tow. The patient hisses oxygen out of the sides of her mask and looks bedraggled.

The sister on the Covid side is irritated by their unheralded appearance and I hear her tell the ambulance crew that they will have to keep the patient in the back of the ambulance until a bed opens. Had we known that they were coming, we could have hastened an admission, but now there is no available bed in the ED.

I can see that the paramedic is not impressed, but the bottom line is that we don't have anywhere to move the patient over from the stretcher. And it is really hot outside, so the air-conditioned ambulance is better than standing in the sun outside the double doors.

The hissing lady is reloaded, and we start to make a space for her. Her family talks to her through the porthole window and the paramedic sits on the grass, looking at his phone.

I'm so over this virus. And I see, to my annoyance, that the next patient to be seen swallowed an overdose of hand sanitiser.

There is a steady increase of people deliberately self-harming by drinking hand sanitiser. Made mostly of alcohol, it can also contain ethyl alcohol or methanol, both of which are toxic. Ingestion can lead to seizures, blindness or even death.

I usually call the poison centre for any accidental or intentional toxin ingestion, but I know this one by heart by now. Today's customer refuses to tell me why he drank the sanitiser. He just stares over my shoulder at the wall, while his employer produces bottle after empty bottle from a shopping bag.

He drank them all.

He will need to be admitted to ICU for multiple blood tests and observation. Once we are sure that there is no physical damage done by the sanitiser, he will be passed along to the psychiatrist, who will help him figure out why he felt compelled to drink it. But he is not on medical aid and the government hospitals are over-subscribed at present.

After making about twenty calls, I find him a bed and move along to the next file. This patient was dashing around, tidying her house for Christmas evening drinks. She was barefoot and, nestled in the deep pile of a shag carpet, was a cocktail stick. Slightly thicker than a toothpick, and lethally sharp on both sides, it is now nestling in the sole of her foot. She hops into the ED, her face streaked with tears.

I can see a mark where the stick has broken on to the underside of her foot. I can feel the other point just under the skin on the back of her foot. The cocktail stick must have gone right between the long bones of her foot and is tenting the skin on the top. She, too, has no medical aid and so palming the removal of the cocktail stick off on the orthopaedic surgeon in theatre is not going to happen.

An x-ray is of no value, as wood is not radio opaque. Not that I need an x-ray, as I can feel the tip moving under the skin when I press on her sole. The problem is that the base of the cocktail stick has broken right off, so there is nothing to grab. I will have to cut down on it to grasp it.

The sole of the foot is a very tender spot for injections. The lady snatches her foot back involuntarily each time I prick it. I must get the sister to hold her foot down so that I can deaden the skin, and then work my way deeper. I put local anaesthetic all along the imagined tract of the toothpick and then cut down around the base. Blood wells up and it is hard to see what I am doing. I use a curved forceps called a mosquito and advance it, spreading the tissues with the opening tips, then grasping hopefully.

Deeper and deeper we go. I can see that the tip wobbles and bobs with each attempt, but the grasper comes back empty. I am now a few centimetres into the sole of her foot, and I am reluctant to grab and pull on invisible things that may be tendons or vital structures inside her foot.

I am about to give up when I feel a firmness between the pincers of the forceps. I click the ratchet to keep the grip and slowly retreat.

Out comes the cocktail stick. I hold it up, triumphant. Victory is ours; money is saved, and patience won out in the end.

I put the bloody little cocktail stick in a specimen jar so that the patient can save it for show and tell.

Twenty

25 December 2021

The snoopies get specially decorated Christmas biscuits this morning. I am working my usual six to two, but they know something unusual is afoot. It is a misty morning, and they seem ethereal on the lawn, black and brindle hovercraft zooming in the half-light.

Blu snoopy, the most recent adoption, shoots away if I make a sudden movement. He circles wide, watching me with almond eyes, and approaches warily from the front. He is so jumpy and yet never aggressive with fear. He wants to believe that the world is not as bad as it has been for him so far.

He is hopeful.

I drive to work wondering if excitement is linked to youth. There used to be a special thrill around Christmas and New Year, a kind of humming energy. Now I am just thankful that there is less traffic on the road.

I can't recall being enthralled by anything for a very long time.

When I got my first motorcycle, I used to leap out of bed to look at it in the morning and stare at it through the window at night. I rode it every moment I could, and I absolutely loved everything about it. I loved how the seat felt under me, the smell of new paint and the smooth purr of the engine. I do not recall being as thrilled by my first car, and now my motorcycle, significantly upgraded from my first 'nifty fifty', stands gathering dust. It seems a hassle to ride it, yet I recall my younger self, so eager to take anything for a spin.

Now it is too hot in summer, too cold in winter, too wet if it rains. I have turned into such a bore.

Watching the snoopies run flat out makes me happy; but it is edged in sadness. I want to laugh out loud in delight; but it also brings tears to my eyes as I cannot erase the transience of youth and health. I see them get stiffer and slower, milky with cataracts. The years rush by until they get left behind, and I have only their precious memories to carry in my heart. All these years and my heart has never overflowed. It just expands, getting heavier and deeper as time passes.

I think of a documentary about Bruce Springsteen where he sings a song 'I'll meet you in my dreams'. I watch the fields scroll by and find the song on my phone. Turn it up to blow the thoughts away.

Jaded, is the word that comes to mind. Too many responsibilities; the world seems a bleak place and the relentlessness of the ED made me somehow smaller than I should have been.

Despite a slow morning, I receive a testicular torsion, a dislocated shoulder and lots of coughing people for Christmas.

I hope that I don't get coronavirus. I didn't put it on my wish list.

We manage to rescue the testicle, partly because a stray urologist comes to the ED for a corona test. I don't know him well, but I have seen him around and I ask him if he is the new urologist.

'Yes,' he says, greeting me politely.

'Pleased to meet you,' I tell him. 'Could you help us with a torsion?'

'You are joking, hey?' he asks. He was literally just passing through. I suppose he finds it bizarre that I just happened to have a patient with a twisted testicle about which I had done nothing until he randomly showed up. The truth is that I had literally just hung up the telephone from discussing said testicle with the radiologist, who had come in from home to do an urgent sonar.

The urologist glances at the clock. 'I will have to find an anaesthetist, and I have prayers at noon.'

I think that most urologists cannot resist a torsion. It trumps feeling prostates and dealing with incontinence, hands down. He steps up to the line, taking the boy immediately to theatre so that he can untwist the testicle and restore the blood supply. He pops past at lunchtime to tell me that it pinked up well and that he is optimistic about its survival. He is still in time for prayers and the boy got to keep both testicles for Christmas.

It is a win all around.

Close to home time, a massive paramedic wheels a tiny lady into the unit. She is as frail as a sparrow, all skin and wrinkles, and is definitely north of ninety. She is clutching her handbag in her lap and dabbing a tissue to her eyes. I intercept them in the corridor and ask what is wrong. She tells me that her family don't want her anymore and they have all gone away for Christmas. They do it every year; send her into the hospital so that they can be rid of her.

The paramedic looks sympathetic as he helps her over to the bed, his massive biceps bulging despite her being as light as a feather. He straightens the blanket under her chin and wishes her well.

'Thank you so much for your help,' she says weepily. 'Before you go,' she blinks wistfully up at him, 'could you look through my handbag? My wristwatch is so precious to me, and they may have taken it. It is very valuable.'

She gazes at him, her knight in shining armour.

'Sure,' the paramedic is happy to oblige and opens the zipper. He rummages around for a bit and comes out with a tiny gold watch face on a very tired leather strap. 'Here you are ma'am,' he says kindly, bending over her.

Quick as a flash, she snatches the watch from him and twines her free hand into the front of his shirt. 'Come here!' she commands, her voice now guttural and sinister. 'Open your mouth. Gotta take your temperature!'

The surprise on the paramedic's face turns to horror as she tries to force the tatty leather watch strap into his mouth. He turns his head away, but she perseveres.

'Open!' she commands, clinging to his shirt as he backs away. She is a wizened limpet, holding fast, when her daughter comes into the unit with her file.

'Mom,' she admonishes, 'please leave that nice man alone. My mother is confused,' she adds, turning to me. 'She keeps trying to take everyone's temperature. You are lucky we got the rectal thermometer away from her,' she tells the paramedic. 'When she assaulted my grandson with the Nazareth star from the top of the tree, we called 911.'

Everything is not as it seems, I think to myself, as I check the boxes for blood and urine and radiology for the Christmas Granny. Getting old is not for sissies.

We have invited friends and a few stragglers for a late lunch. Only six people, who will be placed at wide intervals under the huge shade trees in the garden.

The snoopies love visitors. New laps onto which they can press their long noses; fresh hands to touch their silky ears. And, of course, there is the smell of potato bake and turkey in the oven. They curl up in the kitchen, craftily positioned, in case something slips to the floor.

I find greyhounds to be food thieves in general and so we cannot leave anything unattended. It doesn't help that they are eye level to the kitchen countertop, and that most of them have spent a good portion of their lives starving. Yesterday, the red snoopy ate a whole roast chicken in a few seconds, right out of the pan.

They are also very accident-prone, with too much gas, no brakes, and no fat to cushion themselves. Their sleek skin tears so easily and I am regularly stitching them up after collisions with gate posts and tree trunks. As a breed, they also seem pretty good at howling with very little provocation. Luckily, there are no collisions nor howling today, just bottomless pits for love absorption.

We dish up at the farm table and take our plates and glasses of bubbly into the garden. Everyone has a story of someone that they know with Covid-19. I feel like a hypocrite, as I have spent my whole day with definite Covid pneumonia patients. In fact, I have spent the better part of my year with them. I listen to their chests, take their blood and have even done CPR on some. I change and shower as soon as I get home, but still.

I am surprised that people are not a whole lot more wary of me than they seem to be.

Twenty-One

27 December 2020

It is tradition that the snoopies get a story read to them on Sunday evenings.

I have some funny video footage of my teaching Brown Dog to read. She was sitting on my lap, wearing my reading glasses, and moving her nose obligingly as my finger swept along the lines.

The greyhounds are too big to sit on my lap and they are too noble to admit that they cannot read, so they just lie about in the glowing evening light and listen.

Today's Sunday story is about snakes and how Pookie just used up another of his nine lives.

When I got home, the farm was hot and sleepy. A perfect Sunday afternoon for a huge rinkhals to make its way onto the verandah. As I drove in, the dogs ran down to greet me. I heard Pookie barking like crazy and stepped out of the car to see the rinkhals standing, hood stretched wide, bobbing and weaving as Pookie danced around it. It was close enough to see its glassy eyes, black as coal. A flattened, snub nose flared into a wide hood, dangerously concave as the snake prepared to strike. It shimmered in the afternoon sun like the surface of a wave hanging in the breath of the break. Two cream bands, like handkerchiefs tied at its throat, flagged its identity.

Pookie feinted in and out; too close to the fat coil of danger but too far from me to intervene.

I screamed his name with such desperation that he turned back towards me, just as the snake struck. It missed his shoulder by centimetres. Fumbling with my keys, I opened the front door, calling the dogs and herding them in.

Jake, the prime, red snoopy, jumped right over the top of the rinkhals, clearing it by half a metre. The snake struck again at the leaping shadow, but Jake was far out of reach. It lay flat for a moment, then stood again, hissing in fury. A tongue flickered beneath the beady eyes and the snake stood as tall as my knee.

Another snoopy bounded past. I opened the front door and she shot in. A quick count confirmed that I had them all. Greyhounds lack Pookie's terrier instinct, so they collected gracefully inside the house and lay down on their cushions. Pookie ran up and down the windows, bouncing onto the sills and barking like mad.

Once I had them in and had called the local snake catcher, I could breathe again.

I literally had chest pain, radiating down both of my arms and my hands were shaking as I checked all the dogs for bites. Mercifully there were none, although Pookie had quite a bit of venom on his shoulder. Rinkhals are accurate spitters and lethal biters. I washed him in the basin and told him off for almost being killed.

Alida sends him voice messages all the time; it simply wouldn't do for him to die on my watch.

I tell the story to the snoopies, full of warning and scolding, and they stare silently back at me. I hope that they pay heed. I tell them that I love them and want them to stay out of harm's reach. Pookie lies on the golden grass and watches the world with his slightly slanted eyes. They are more turquoise in colour now and, with his luminous caramel coat, he would make a fine item of jewellery.

The evening is a rich gold and emerald green, and the darkness comes on soft feet. The sunset is iridescent, and the valley is magnificently bruised. I don't feel like moving so I sit on the lawn until the dew settles around me and mosquitoes start to sting.

I mull over the past year, when we thought a three-week lockdown was a long time. And the first wave, when we thought that we were swamped with patients. I wonder what we would have done differently if we had known what was coming.

I wish that I could tell what is going to happen next. It is exhausting not to know. To spend most of my workday scurrying around like a well-trained mouse in a novel maze. Whiskers, like intuition, working overtime as I try to ascertain which way to turn. Sensing danger, but then left turns to right and the world is upside down.

I am Alice down the rabbit hole, with fevered imaginings and real dangers.

The last light has shimmered away and now it is full dark. I gather the snoopies and Pookie and put them to bed.

Tomorrow I will be back on the battlefront. Best I get some sleep.

Twenty-Two

1 January 2021

I drew the short straw for the New Year's Eve shift. Luckily for me, alcohol is banned again, and the shift only has corona customers. No stabbings, no shootings, no drunk driving. No hands blown off by fireworks.

Just many, many feverish people, coughing and grunting behind various curtains.

At last, the eastern horizon lightens and we emerge, drenched, from the darkness. It is the tension of the change that pulls me forwards and the closing of the circle that makes me whole.

I sit on the shirking wall and watch the day creep in. There is certainly no crack in the dawn; nothing sharp or sudden in the change. Perhaps it should be called the seep of dawn.

I have been delaying repeating my haemoglobin level because it remains low and so I have gone into a stage of denial. But I force myself to go down to the laboratory as a New Year's resolution and offer my arm to the friendly vampire.

A few hours later, my phone pings with the result. It is still dismally low. I decide not to think about it again for a while. My body seems to have adapted to the low levels and I no longer feel light headed and short of breath.

Sometimes I feel like I have seen it all. But even after thirty years in the ED, I still learn something new every day. And sometimes the universe seems so beautiful, despite the gruesome twists of fate.

There is a strange euphoria to finishing a night shift. Fatigue and relief make a heady mix. I gather the greyhounds for a super-long walk. We go along the edge of the field and onwards through the overgrown farmland.

The tall grass bobs and waves in the wind, parting like hair on the hillside. The seed is pink and purple and gently furry on the tips.

We walk for miles, the snoopies content to stay on the path which winds through the green valley like a bald brown snake. They walk ahead of me and behind me, their coats gleaming blacks and brindles in the early light.

A deserted New Year's Day in the valley, we follow a small river. Acacia boughs, thick with nests, dip to touch the water. The greyhounds wade in, lying down in the dappled shallows.

I consider filling my water bottle from the crystal water, but I am put off by the memory of a patient who came to the Professor complaining of difficulty swallowing. She sent him for a barium swallow, which showed the classic 'rat's tail' sign of a tumour in the oesophagus. She needed to do a biopsy to establish if this was cancer and the biopsy would be taken via a gastroscope.

When she put the scope into his oesophagus, she dislodged the leech that had attached there and was masquerading as a tumour. The patient must have swallowed a baby leech when drinking contaminated water. He was from a rural area and the leech had feasted and fattened until it prevented him from swallowing anything and forced him to seek medical attention.

The site of the leech's attachment bled so much that the patient almost died under anaesthetic. Leeches have an anticoagulant in their saliva, and we could not stop the bleeding through the endoscope.

Luckily for the patient, the Professor had specialised in oesophageal surgery. The oesphagus is a very sensitive pipe and does not appreciate interference. If you make a hole in it, gastric acid leaks into the chest and this has a dismal outcome. The Professor had done her research and found that the single most important factor determining success in oesphageal surgery was the patient's blood pressure during the surgery.

She kept her beady blue eyes on the blood pressure machine, but her anaesthetist got wise to her interference and turned the monitor away from the surgical field. The Professor was undeterred by the repositioning of the monitors and simply walked around the anaesthetist to see the vital signs.

'The blood pressure is too low,' she announced.

'The blood pressure is fine,' the anaesthetist countered. She should have known better.

'It is too low,' the Professor stopped operating.

I could see that the anaesthetist was flustered by the turn of events that had changed a twenty-minute gastroscopy into an eight-hour open oesophageal repair. 'Why don't you mind your own business?' she asked.

I could not believe my ears.

The Professor froze.

'As the surgeon, the blood pressure is my business.'

There was no counterargument to that, and the anaesthetist gave the patient some adrenaline to increase his blood pressure.

I suspected that she would be looking for another list soon.

When the patient woke up in recovery the Professor told him the good news that he did not have cancer. The bad news was that he had a scar from his chin to his pubis, making a little detour around his belly button.

The water looks so tempting and I don't even know if we have leeches in Gauteng, but I am not going to chance it.

We walk to the edge of a rocky gorge. Trees spill down the ravine like silent monks, their hooded heads bowed in the lazy heat. Reaching the edge, the river gasps and plunges downwards. A thousand dizzy drops echo against the sheer walls, an endless clattering cheer.

We stand at the head of the ravine for a while before turning for home. The river will continue, twisting back and pushing forward, swollen and urgent, it will drive towards the distant roar of the ocean.

At the journey's end, the river will be lost to what it becomes.

My feet are burning as the morning's euphoria wears off. The world shimmers flat and silver, my shadow pressed smaller beneath my shabby boots. All I feel like is a swim and resting in the deep shade of the stoep. Later a glass of red wine, loads of ice-cold water, and early to bed.

The greyhounds don't mind.

Twenty-Three

4 January 2021

It is still us.

The same team of doctors and nurses for nine whole months. Leave is cancelled and I am beginning to feel like a caged animal. We are all thinner and greyer and worn down by the pandemic. We are hunched at our posts while the storm rages around us. No question, this wave is worse than the first. The patients are much sicker, and there are so many more of them. The clinical picture is different too, with a totally new demographic of people dying from the virus.

It is as if coronavirus was taken back to the lab for a tune up and racing tweak. Turbo and free-flow exhausts fitted, it's back on the street.

Not that I am a conspiracy theorist, on any level.

So far, no staff has abandoned the ship and no patients have been turned away. The ICU has sixty Covid patients with thirty-four on ventilators.

We are tired and the romance is over.

I hear that there are almost 22 000 new cases diagnosed over the past twenty-four hours. It feels like half of them have come through the ED, although realistically I know that I have only seen thirty-two today. Three needed CPR, though, and that is an intimate act to ask of me when you are shedding clouds of virus.

I can only hold my breath for so long.

The next patient is a young man with a high temperature and shortness of breath. If I hear one more patient with an incessant, hacking cough, I might cut my own throat. He had a positive Covid-19 test eighteen days ago. This is a strange presentation, as usually the pneumonia shows up on about day eight, but he has low oxygen levels and a dreadful x-ray. I snap up the last ICU bed for him; but when I look on my app, I cannot find his Covid result. I re-check the spelling of his surname and look under his identity number.

Nothing.

I go back to the door of his room.

'Which laboratory did you test with?' I ask. 'I cannot find your result anywhere.'

He looks sheepish.

'I actually didn't test,' he tells me. 'My girlfriend tested eighteen days ago. She was positive, so I thought I was too.'

I am flummoxed. I can't send him to ICU with Covid pneumonia if I don't have documented proof that he is positive. There are no PUI beds. The swab is going to take six hours if we absolutely rush it. And, after almost three weeks, it may well be negative already.

I stare at the Eighteen Day Cougher. What am I supposed to do with him? Why would he actively lie and tell the triage sister and nursing staff that he had tested when he had not? We now have him on the Covid 'side' of the ED, with all the other short of breath, coughing people, and he may not have the virus after all.

'Tjoh,' the sister says, shaking her head. I am also amazed.

I suppose I will have to keep him in the ED until the swab comes back or a PUI bed opens up. His chest x-ray looks like definite Covid, but I need the PCR as proof.

I am distracted by a woman's voice in the triage room.

'I think that my husband is having a stroke!'

I can hear the panic in her voice.

Possible strokes, like chest pain, are triaged as a priority one and must come through immediately. Almost ninety per cent of strokes are clots that get lodged in the blood supply to the brain, and if you catch them early enough you can give medication to thin the blood and hopefully dissolve the clot. Ten per cent of strokes bleed into the brain, for which there is seldom any active treatment. Bleeds into the tissue of the brain have a poor outcome, but time is of the essence for clots; if you can dissolve them before there is too much damage, it can be a game changer. I see the husband being bundled into a wheelchair and hustled to an open bed. The wife stays behind to open the file.

'Hi,' I say to the maybe stroke.

'Hiya Doc,' he answers with a goofy grin.

Doesn't look like a stroke so far.

'What's happening?' I ask, my pen poised.

'Took some benzos,' he answers, his smile widening and his mask drooping off his ear.

'Is it prescription medication?' I ask.

'Yeah … just …' he drifts off for a few seconds, '… six.'

I get him to hold up his legs and arms, touch his finger to mine and then his own nose and ask a few more questions. Aside from slurred speech and drowsiness, there is not much to find.

His wife arrives at the bedside in a flurry of nerves. I ask her for the history from her perspective.

'Well, obviously, he's having a stroke. I mean, this is not how he usually is. He can't stand up or speak properly!'

'He told me that he took six sleeping tablets this morning.' I tell her.

'No way!'

She holds my gaze for a few seconds and then turns to him, hands on her hips. 'Babe?'

The goofy grin is back.

'Yep.' Like the cat who got the cream, he almost licks his lips.

She turns back to me and shakes her head emphatically. 'No

way,' she says to me, as if Goofy and I have secretly made up this history in order to hide an evolving stroke.

'Well, that is the story that he told me and, clinically, the picture is one of an overdose, whether it was intentional or not.' I turn to him. 'Were you trying to harm yourself?'

'Nah.'

I believe him.

'So,' I continue, 'we can take some blood tests and send him for an MRI of his brain, but I am not sure that it is necessary.'

The wife unequivocally wants the investigations and so I arrange them.

I see the Eighteen Day Cougher being pushed along the corridor towards us. He is groaning and coughing non-stop. He is radiating germs; I can almost see them in a teeming green cloud around him. Goofy's smile dims and his wife stares in horror as the Cougher gets parked in the bay right next door. He has to be moved from the Covid side because we do not have a definite positive result. There is not even a curtain between them. There is nowhere else to stash the Cougher while management decides what to do with him.

I suggest that we break with protocol and send Goofy to MRI on a wheelchair with his wife at the helm. That way, we can get him out of here with minimal exposure.

They jump at the chance; Goofy even boosting himself briskly off the bed and into the waiting chair.

It is ridiculous and scary but also just a tiny bit funny.

Of course, all Goofy's tests are normal aside from a raised benzodiazepine level.

Goofy's wife is so relieved that he is not having a stroke that she buys milkshakes for all the staff. I notice that she did not get one for him. He is going to have to give her some answers, I suspect, but I am releived that all is well.

By the time that they get back from MRI, I have managed to find a PUI bed for the Cougher, so everyone is safely distributed, and I can go home to Alida and the snoopies.

Hallelujah.

Twenty-Four

10 January 2021

The numbers are still worsening statistically, but it feels to me like the tide may be about to turn. Working in the ED is like standing in the full force of a storm, just beyond where the waves have swallowed up everything in their path. The saltwater spray lashes you and the world is reduced to the roaring sea.

If you are watching and waiting for the turn, you might feel the slight ebb in the water rushing the shore, a slight easing in the fury of the wind. An almost imperceptible change in the energy.

The eye of the storm, my mother would say.

I smile to myself. She was always the pessimist. And here I am, in my mask and gown, holding thumbs.

There are no ventilators available at present. The physician group sends a message to ask us to call them if we have a patient who potentially needs a ventilator. There is an ethics committee set up to make difficult decisions about who will get ventilated and who will not. We need to make that decision before the ED intubates and initiates ventilation, because once they are on, they cannot be swapped out for a younger patient with a better prognosis.

Once it is set up, that is their ventilator until they get better or die.

I see on the WhatsApp groups that there are no beds available in Gauteng at present. There are step-down oxygen and isolation facilities at the NASREC field hospital, but no beds for the sicker patients.

One of the radiologists pops past the ED to ask me a pertinent question. 'So, if the doctors or nurses get sick, will the hospital have a bed for them?'

Quite a few health care workers have asked me this question, and I think that the answer is that they might not. I cannot see that a hospital which is creaking at the seams will have a side ward all set up in case one of their own needs it.

Would I keep a bed if I were in charge? My initial thought was no, but as the pandemic unfolds, I am changing my mind. Now, I think I would keep a room aside and I would make it a very nice room indeed. So many of my colleagues have stood their ground in the line of fire and earned my honest respect I have realised how undervalued we all are.

You can have all the ventilators and ICUs in the world; without health care workers, you will have nothing.

So, yes. If I were in charge, a fellow soldier would get the best treatment.

I am rolling my chair from wall to wall, planning the colour of the duvet in the dedicated ward, when my favourite physician pops his head around the door: 'We are OK for now for ventilators. Got six available this morning. Quick clean for four of them and new patients on already; but I still have two open.'

I stop rolling the chair. 'Six ventilators became available in the course of one morning?'

I doubt that the hospital bought six new ventilators, so that leaves only two options. I raise my eyebrows inquiringly. He nods his head. 'Terrible virus, this,' is his parting shot. He moves quickly and is never one for chit chat.

How depressing.

Twenty-Five

22 January 2021

Yesterday, the medical rescue helicopter crashed. The crew was the ECMO team, specialists in putting patients onto a complex heart and lung bypass called extracorporeal membrane oxygenation. They were on their way to collect a patient dying of Covid pneumonia, when something went wrong and the chopper disappeared in a ball of flame.

The team was based at Milpark but the members worked regularly at many hospitals, as well as ours, and we knew them well.

The ED arranges an impromptu memorial for six in the morning. We gather in our ambulance bay and our lead physician says a few words. We sing and bow our heads. I look around the silent group. These people are my family. There are more grey heads than dark or fair now; candles illuminating their faces in the half light.

We are depleted.

Not only are skills and friends lost, but our spirit is eroded. This pandemic has worn us down, slowly bankrupting our resolve, until we are like husks of our former selves.

There is a beautiful wreath where the chopper would have landed and a small stand with pictures of the doctors, nurse, paramedic and pilot who are gone, each leaving gaping spaces.

Grim has been busy and the barrage of loss seems endless.

The prayer session ends, and my colleagues disperse into smaller groups. Many are still holding candles; some are openly weeping, others consoling. I stand in the somber stillness and wonder how we can grow from this.

Is it true that losing one's life while attempting to save another is the ultimate act of love? I have often thought that a parent's love is the purest part of humanity, but saving your own offspring is, perhaps, also a way of saving yourself. Saving a stranger's life – at the cost of your own – is a different story.

Of course, the ECMO team did not know that they would die yesterday. I'm sure that they had all entertained the possibility of the helicopter crashing, but probably put it aside as highly unlikely.

What they did know is that they would spend a large part of their day in close and intimate contact with a person who has Covid pneumonia. The purpose of their mercy flight was to bypass his heart and lungs at the hospital where he was, which did not have ECMO facilities, and keep him alive for the journey back to Johannesburg.

Who would go to war if they knew the probable outcome? Would they sacrifice their own safety and the wellbeing of their families if death was definite? I think not, but they took the chance, knowing that it was a possibility, and that is courage.

As it happens, the team made the ultimate sacrifice. I cannot dismiss their bravery, and out of respect for them and the countless other health care workers who have died from Covid, I must keep marching.

This is the dedication that Covid asks of us.

I blow out my candle and think of the vitality of that team, extinguished. The fine smoke from the smoldering wick curls up in my nose, reminding me of the tinkle and chatter of a dinner party. The clinking of glasses and the deep fill of friendship.

They were all so young; they had their whole life ahead of them. So many sunsets and night skies that they will not see.

I find myself increasingly aware of my own mortality. Strange thoughts flit into my mind, like what music I would like at my funeral. Mariage D'armour and Air on G string, definitely, and maybe Canon in D.

On second thoughts, I dip my candle into the flame flickering at the wreath and take it into the ED. I hope the smoke detectors don't catch its scent, but I need the warmth of this bobbing light today.

We also hear that Minister Jackson Mthembu, the government spokesperson on Covid and other matters, has died of Covid. He was only sixty-two and was a splendid example of what a politician in an ideal world should be.

Our world is far from ideal. I wonder when or how this pandemic will end, and how much longer we can keep this up.

Every day is an act of bravery.

A man hobbles past our little memorial and in through the double doors. He has a plastic bag tied around his foot and the inside is filmed with blood.

I follow him to a cubicle and ask him what happened. He tells me that he dropped the edge of a concrete bench on his foot. His small toe is completely severed, attached only by a sliver of skin. It is mashed and rotated and looks nothing like a toe. It cannot be saved. I take a photograph of it and, with his permission, send it to the orthopaedic surgeon. He will need to have it snipped off and properly tidied up in the theatre.

I am working with the Calligrapher today. We have a lot in common, not least is our dark sense of humour. He is sitting in the little office with his array of pens, blowing his careful script dry as he writes. I call him the Calligrapher as he has the most beautiful handwriting and prides himself on perfectly written notes. He is also obsessed with pens and always has an array of rare and interesting colours lined up in his scrubs pocket. Our candle is flickering warmly on the desk, casting a small, wobbly shadow.

I settle on the other chair and call the orthopaedic surgeon to make arrangements. As I finish the call, the cardiologist on call joins us.

'I hear my brother-in-law came in. He hurt his toe.'

I check with the patient, and he is fine to show his photo far and wide. I open it on my mobile and the cardiologist staggers back in horror.

'Oh, my goodness,' he gasps, with visible pallor. 'That looks terrible!'

Recovering his composure, he tells me that his brother-in-law is a very wealthy man who owns a castle in France.

In unison, the Calligrapher and I say '... but he only has nine toes!' And we cackle like a pair of jackals.

The cardiologist tells us that we have a macabre sense of humour. This, we know. He still looks a bit queasy but manages to greet his brother-in-law and stand in the corner while we get him ready for theatre.

I have my back to him while I am dressing the toe. I hear him take a deep breath and I know what is coming. When people feel faint, they sigh just before they go down. I glance at him and see the tell-tale pallid sheen around his eyes.

'Lie down on the floor,' I tell him.

'I'm fine,' he assures me.

I abandon the dressing just as his eyes roll back. I put my arms around his waist and grab his belt and his body slumps against me like a drunken dancer. We make quite a thud, first against the bed and then the floor. The Calligrapher hurries into the room.

The cardiologist grunts and makes a few little convulsing movements and then wakes up slowly and stares up at us: the Calligrapher, his brother-in-law and me. Three concerned faces and the hospital ceiling in the background. I can see he is trying to put this all together.

'You had a vaso vagal,' I tell him. This is medical speak for people who faint at the sight of blood. It is a real condition, where the heart slows down, and the blood pressure drops. Aside from lying down, there is not much that you can do about it. But if you feel it coming on, often with clammy skin and ringing in your ears, you can lie down and put your feet up, to redistribute the blood flow to your brain.

Some people still pass out, though.

I remember a guy who had a dislocated shoulder who begged me not to put up a drip. He told me that he fainted at the very thought of a needle. I could not reduce his shoulder without sedation, so I eventually talked him into it. As the needle pierced his skin, he said, 'I'm not feeling good.' I had him on a monitor and his heart slowed down until it stopped for a few seconds. He lost consciousness, even though he was lying down. I was about to start CPR when his heart started beating again.

His phobia of needles had literally stopped his heart.

The cardiologist tells me that he has never fainted before in the presence of gruesomeness. I hope that it doesn't happen again, especially not while he is doing an angiogram or some other life-saving intervention.

Twenty-Six

10 February 2021

The good news is that the Corona numbers are going down. There are still quite a few cases, but nothing like the chaos a month ago.

The bad news is that we are back to loadshedding. Rolling blackouts have made a comeback and we are all depressed about what this means about the future of our country. I am sure that, somewhere in the system, a doctor is writing about the medical ramifications of power outages.

Aside from the obvious ones, like home oxygen concentrators running flat and people falling in the dark, I have a growing list of load shedding injuries. There are house fires from untended candles, broken fingers from the pull starter on generators and traffic accidents as the traffic signals are dead. Today I have a lady who got an electric shock from trying to switch over from the main power to the generator.

'It is not the shock, though, that's bothering me,' she tells me. 'My six-year-old son hit me with the broomstick.'

'Why did he do that?' I ask, intrigued.

'I was astounded, myself, until he told me that he had learned it on a first aid course. I think that they tell first aiders not to touch an electrocution victim but to rather push them away from the source of the electricity with something that does not conduct. A broom is ideal and somehow my son understood that the treatment for electric shock is a sharp jab or blow with a broomstick.'

She shows me a tram-track bruise across her thighs. I am amazed. Her son took that lesson to heart, it seems.

I ask the nurse to do an ECG just to check that the shock has had no effect on the rhythm of her heart, and I write her a script for a painkiller. I glance through the triage doors and see a sick-looking man in the waiting room. He is groaning and half-slithering off his chair. 'I am really ill,' I hear him tell the triage sister. 'I feel terrible. I need to lie down.'

The triage sister brings him through and instals him on a bed. His file will follow.

I stand at the bottom of the bed and start to write his history. He is thirty-two years old and previously well. He hit his head while playing football a week ago. A head clash when two players jumped for the ball. He had a mild headache and then, two days later, he started vomiting. He thought he was concussed. Now he has uncontrollable rigours and body pain. His temperature is north of thirty-nine and he is shivering and moaning under a heavy jacket.

No travel history. No previous illnesses. No chronic medication. No loss of consciousness with the head injury.

Well, we will start with my new best friend, corona. Let's get a rapid test for the antigen and a portable chest x-ray. I don't want to send him down to the x-ray department and expose everyone enroute. With that high temperature, he definitely has an infection of some sort. I think that the head injury is a red herring.

His chest x-ray is clear and the Covid antigen is negative.

I examine him and his abdomen is tight as a drum. Even light pressure and his muscles spasm. Called peritonitis, it is a rigidity that tells me that something – blood or digestive fluid – is irritating his inner linings.

I found this a difficult concept to grasp until I had actually seen the inside of the abdomen as a medical student. From the outside there is skin, fat, muscle and then an inner membrane, or peritoneum, that surrounds the organs. It is a complex affair of pockets within pockets, but the bottom line is that the organs and intestines should be intact, like a sealed roll of sausage inside a packet. If there is a hole made in the casing of the sausage, then the mince escapes and makes a dreadful mess inside the packet.

So it is with the human body. The air and digestive products are sealed in a tube that runs one end to the other. If there is a tear in the tube or an organ, the air or fluid leaks out and irritates the peritoneum.

This patient's abdomen is stiff as a board. He has peritonitis.

I ask him if he still has his appendix. He says that he does, and I include it as a possibility in my investigations. A burst appendix could easily be the cause of his symptoms, although it is strange that he did not volunteer the information that he has a pain in his stomach. When I touch the area overlying his appendix, he almost leaps off the bed, but he did not mention abdominal pain beforehand.

His infective markers are massively raised, and his CT scan is very suggestive of appendicitis. The appendix is thickened, and fluid filled, with stranding and inflammation all around it.

I call Blue Eyes and he appears in the ED to see the patient. We have worked together for years and have an excellent relationship. He is one of very few colleagues that I see socially. His passion for animals is endearing as is his sense of humour and perspective

He is not convinced that the patient has acute appendicitis but agrees to admit him and start him on antibiotics. Even after strong medication in the drip, the patient still looks and feels terrible. We will also get the physician involved, but the surgeon agrees that there is something happening in the abdomen. He is reluctant to rush into surgery, especially because the patient's platelets are low, and this might cause him to bleed excessively.

We agree that the patient has septic shock, which is a dangerous state of affairs when an infection overwhelms the immune system and causes problems with clotting, low blood pressure and often ends in multi-organ failure.

Somewhere in the middle of the night, my phone pings with a message from Blue Eyes. He wants to know if I did blood cultures. The patient has deteriorated, and they have put him on a ventilator. I did request blood cultures before we started the antibiotic and I look them up on my lab app and send them to him. They will not be of much use, because the result is not ready yet, but at least he knows that they were done.

Blue Eyes sends me back a picture of the most dreadful rash. The patient is covered in it. This kind of rash is called purpura and it means that the patient is bleeding under the skin. It is sinister and dark purple with maroon accents. Characteristically, it does not go white, or blanche, when a glass is rolled over it.

It is a very bad sign.

By now I am wide awake and really alarmed. 'Meningococcal?' I message back immediately. I have only seen a rash like that once in my life and it did not bode well. It had been on a teenager who died within the hour from bacterial meningitis.

'Don't know.' He writes back. I think back about the history that the patient gave. He did say that he had a headache after he bumped his head, but it only lasted a day and that was a week ago. Meningococcal meningitis is a rapidly progressive illness; usually a day or less from onset of symptoms to time of death. By the time the patient is in septic shock from meningitis, they will be obtunded.

I am also thinking about haemorrhagic fevers like Ebola or Myberg. There has been an outbreak in Guinea but, as far as I know, no cases in South Africa.

Now, of course, I must google each of these viruses and remind myself about them all. What hideous things they are, viewed under an electron microscope. They look like hooks of thickened wire. Menacing, for sure. I might as well get up and make a cup of tea as I am not going to get back to sleep anytime soon.

To me, browsing is something that herbivores do. But I am

increasingly reliant on the internet to keep up with evolving knowledge, and to remind myself of things that I used to know. I sit at the kitchen table and scroll through the group of germs called arborviruses. I thought that they were named after the French word for tree, being more common in jungles or tropical areas, but that arborvirus is an acronym for arthropod borne viruses.

Next, I need to google which arthropods carry the various viruses.

It turns out mosquitos, fleas, ticks, flies and mites are all arthropods. Blue Eyes messages again. He is sorry to tell me that the patient has just passed away. He thinks that we should all take preventative antibiotics because whatever germ this was, it blasted a previously healthy young man into Grim's arms in less than six hours from admission.

I widen my internet search to include typhus and other rickettsia. I stop when I get to chiggers, which are microscopic mites that feed on the actual skin of their host, rather than suck their blood. They are different to jiggers, which are sand fleas that feed on blood.

There are so many opportunists out there. I put my phone back on charge and make another cup of tea.

The night is thick and dark, and we are deep in the witching hour. The fever tree in the courtyard scratches on the tin roof of the little farmhouse and the inky landscape stretches out around me like a blanket. A few hours before dawn, the stars are bright and cold, and the moon droops in the west. It looks like someone squashed it between their fingers and left it orange and oblong.

It feels like the world of uber germs is closing in on me. That poor guy. I feel terrible for him and for his family. I also feel terrible for Blue Eyes. For all his macho general surgeon-ness, he admits all his patients into his heart as well as into his ward.

Twenty-Seven

28 February 2021

Speaking of surgeons, the Professor is brought into the ED on a stretcher. Despite being covered with a blanket and a mask, I would know those sharp eyes anywhere.

'Is it you?' I ask, as the stretcher comes in from the ambulance bay.

She looks slightly perplexed, and I reflect that it is a bit of a dumb question.

We have not seen each other in years, and I am wearing a mask and a hood. I assist her by introducing myself to the paramedics. They tell me that their patient is a medical doctor and a professor. 'I know,' I say, taking her hands in mine. 'This is my professor!'

Despite Covid, I lean down and hug her.

The staff gathers round to meet the famous Professor. They show her great respect and deference. It is so wonderful to see her again that I almost forget to ask her why she is here.

Our reunion is quite tearful. Life is too busy and, especially with the pandemic, we have not had a chance to connect in years. She is an icon, and I must remind myself that she must be almost eighty years of age now. She is still regal and sharp as a tack.

Before and after my shifts, I go and sit by her bed. We talk about medical school, where she still teaches, our lives and our shared experiences. I bring her grapes and orange juice and help to connect her television to the movie channel.

Spending time with her is like coming home.

The ED bumbles along with nothing out of the ordinary. The occasional amputated finger and broken leg. Routine children with fevers and people with abdominal pain. A seven-year-old who impersonated an animated character by putting cotton buds in her ears and trying to fly off the top of the wardrobe.

The upswing of her arms drove the buds through her eardrums. It probably seemed like a good idea at the time.

Reconnecting with the Professor brings back so many memories. She tells me earnestly that I was her one true failure. I am surprised, as I think that I did quite well at medical school. Expanding on her statement, she tells me how much she hoped that I would become a surgeon. I am sitting on the edge of her bed as there are no chairs; visitors are not encouraged during Covid. She lifts my hand from my lap and examines it. She tells me that I was a natural when operating and she considered my hands excellent. It is a peculiarly intimate moment and I feel both proud and sad simultaneously. I have a worker's hands, practical and strong, and I do think that I would have been a good surgeon. I am ambivalent about having them examined, though, as I prefer not to be seen.

When I first worked with the Professor, I moonlighted at the government mortuary. I had long considered forensic pathology as a specialty, and I tried it out for six months.

It was the most horrendous job in the world. Surgery was much better for me, but the long hours were ridiculous. The mortuary kept office hours; the dead were seldom in a hurry.

The other doctors working at the morgue were decidedly peculiar and the middle-aged receptionist even more unusual in her staid normality. She was myopic and mild-mannered and seldom said a word. She sewed and crocheted continuously, churning out gaudy covered coat hangers and baby booties by the dozen. She would take her breaks sauntering through the fridges and was adept at any task required.

She seemed not to mind wading through the gruesome tide at all.

My first case was a young man who had supposedly drowned in a Johannesburg lake. It was Christmas time and there were colourful fountains to mark festivities. He was found dead in the water and his body was brought for postmortem. This being my first autopsy, I was assisted by a much older pathologist. He could not have been less interested in the case; we opened and closed in record time and filled in all the documents.

The next day, the drowned man's employer came to the mortuary. The victim had been an excellent swimmer and was not under the influence of alcohol. He wanted a second opinion on the postmortem. I trudged into the fridge and fetched the body. He was sewn up from chin to pubis with a waxy, lace-like thread. I snipped it open and discovered, to my horror, that all the internal organs had been removed. When I closed this patient yesterday, I knew what had been inside. Someone had obviously come back overnight and stolen the organs.

And so began an enquiry that would bring down a ring of people trading in organs. Mortuary workers, security guards and policemen were all involved. It had been going on for years. I suppose that grieving families were only too happy to get the body back for burial; no one checked that the organs were intact. And, even if they had, it might have been justified as part of a postmortem.

People desperate for transplant and shamans had been a willing market; the original owner certainly did not need the organs any longer, and business was booming. I had wondered on my first day how so many entry-level state employees had driven such fancy cars.

It turned out that the power supply to the fountain lights was shorting and electrocuting people in the water. We figured this out when we got a second drowning from the same lake in as many days.

The other memorable case that crossed my path was a young lady who was murdered at a train station east of town. The senior pathologist recognised a pattern and recalled previous cases for comparison.

In retrospect, the first victim of the serial killer had been assessed as a once-off crime. She had been buried, unidentified, after the postmortem. Now the pathologist wanted to revisit her case, which meant that she would have to be exhumed. Depending on the level of decay, they could perhaps link her to a string of crimes and even ascertain her identity. There was a computer program that could age her in three dimensions and give numerous possibilities of how she looked as a child and as an adult.

For the computer to calculate this, we needed the bare bones of her face and skull. As the most junior on the team, I was tasked with this.

I carried the poor lady's head in a packet to the dowdy receptionist. She barely glanced at it, plopping it out of the plastic packet and into a large pot of boiling water. She then continued to crochet a doily to cover her spare toilet roll. It was one of a set; one for the top of the cistern, a little carpet shaped for the base of the toilet and a cover for the seat. She propped the pattern book up and crossed her ankles as the water bubbled away and strands of hair matted on the surface.

To this day, crocheted bathroom sets give me night terrors.

Aside from a fascination with the extent of our capacity for evil, forensic pathology was a depressing, monotonous and foul-smelling specialty. I rejoiced when my six months were over, and I could focus on the warm, pink insides of live people and the quick wit of the Professor.

I think back to those days with a sweet sentimentality. It is fantastic to have the Professor's company again for a few days, and I am both sorry and pleased to see her go home, recovered, by the end of the week.

I am sitting in the ED, reliving those years, while the Calligrapher is eating corn chips. It is the pause between each chip that I find most egregious. Crunch, crunch, crunch. Pause. Hand to the packet. Crackling of paper. Pause. More fiddling, chip snagged, up to the mouth it goes.

Repeat.

Eventually, I can think of nothing else. Even though I have my back to him, I am mesmerised. Sometimes he pauses mid-chew, especially when he reaches a fancy bit of pen work.

Crunch.

Pause.

Crunch, crunch.

I swivel on my chair and meet his eyes. His hand freezes halfway to the packet.

'Sorry,' he mumbles into his mask. 'Would you like a chip?'

I am forced to smile at his earnest apology. He has brown eyes and auburn curls, and it is impossible to get annoyed with him. He spends every free moment eating but remains as thin as a rail.

It is miraculous.

Twenty-Eight

5 MARCH 2021

Today is corona's first anniversary in South Africa.
What a truly terrible year it has been. We may not be in a great place but thank goodness we are not where we were.

The snoopies get special biscuits because it is also my birthday. Alida was going to surprise me with sushi this morning, but I discovered it in the fridge last night and ate it all up.

She also got a huge box of doughnuts for the staff. Despite this, the Calligrapher has already opened his first bag of corn chips.

Sigh.

The vaccination is all the rage on the news, but there is no sign of it for our ED team. Two weeks in, even though I have a voucher and have registered twice on the website, I have not yet been summoned by the powers that be.

To be fair, I am not convinced that I need a vaccine. After a year of seeing hundreds of patients with Covid, I must have some immunity. But I would, at least, like the option. I am feeling increasingly ignored and sidelined.

I also feel that the massive toll that this year has taken on health care workers is hugely under-estimated. Every day I have consultations with nursing staff who beg me to book them off from the Covid ward. Many are suffering from stress-related illnesses. I can give them a few days off and a referral for counselling. I cannot, however, book them off from working with corona patients. I wish that I could, but I can't.

Today I am planning an intricate system whereby any third-wave corona pneumonia victims will be only seen by health care workers who have had the opportunity to be vaccinated.

This seems only fair to me. I am not sure how I will get it right, but I am plotting and scheming away. Wheeling my chair backwards and forwards and keeping rhythm with the crunching of the corn chips. If the Calligrapher notices, he is not deterred.

Bits of corn chip and flakes of doughnut icing crackle under the chair wheels. I gaze longingly out of the double doors and at the Friday afternoon sky.

I am tired and I want to go home.

I think back to *Heart of Darkness*, which I read a long time ago. I recall how the pulsating jungle became a metaphor for innate evil and how gossamer thin the veneer of civilisation is. Who, in fact, were the cannibals and what was the horror that Kurtz refers to at the end? I think it was the horror at his own brutality towards the native people and the elephants that he killed for the ivory trade. Others read it as the fear of the darkness, but I think it is more likely to be fear of what the darkness hides.

A fear of what is out there.

I would like to borrow that powerful tale and bring it a 122 years forward. To the horror I see around me every day. Joseph Conrad saw the Congo as the unknown, the tribes hostile and the river a living threat. So much easier to put a pulsating life into the canopy of jungle than into our familiar shopping centres and workplaces.

And yet the madness resonates.

Some people tell me that the coronavirus pandemic is just a political ploy and they do not believe that it actually exists. No one who has spent one day in an ED or an ICU over the course of the last year would give that a second thought.

Corona is real.

We have a massive computer on which we view x-rays. Double click on the person's name and the chest x-ray fills the screen. Like a slap, one wants to step back in fright. The physicians' eyes used to search the image with real fear, but now they also look defeated.

They look like dogs that have been entered into a fight that they cannot win.

As the violet afternoon sky builds for a storm, I recognise that we all have post traumatic stress disorder. Triggered by witnessing or experiencing a terrifying event, it is a constellation of symptoms, all of which I could check as positive for myself and our whole team. Emotional lability, avoidance, exhaustion, nightmares, tearfulness and free-floating anxiety are all around us.

The wind picks up and the blue-green canopies bow ahead of the slivers of lightning. I wonder if the trees fear which one will be struck. It is the unpredictability of this illness that is making us all crazy: the anticipation, the imagination.

The rain starts to lash the awnings of the ED. I wish that I were home, safe around the fire with Alida and the snoopies. I am tired of this threat and tired of this fight.

Twenty-Nine

11 March 2021

An ambulance crew clatters through the double door. I spy the silver struts of a scoop stretcher under the patient, a special device that unclips head and toe, so that a trauma patient can be lifted or set down without rolling or sliding them.

A red neck collar confirms my first impression that this is a trauma, rather than a medical, patient. His face is covered in blood, but he is awake and talking.

'Hi there,' I greet him as they pass me in the corridor. 'What happened?'

'I was hit by a jet ski.'

This gives me pause. The nearest body of water is about thirty kilometres from this hospital, and it is not a mechanism that I see often. I used to do the occasional locum near the Vaal dam, and we saw many boat and jet ski accidents. Here, not so much.

'A jet ski?' I repeat.

'Yep.' He spits out a few teeth.

The paramedic fills in the details. The patient was waiting in the traffic on a single carriageway and an oncoming vehicle braked suddenly. The other guy had a jet ski on a trailer which was not properly secured. The jet ski shot off the trailer and straight through the patient's windscreen.

What bad luck, I tell him.

Turns out that he has a Le Forte grade three facial fracture. This is a break across the midface, separating the palate from the rest of the skull. It runs through the sinuses and the eye sockets, and it is a nightmare to fix.

I will be handing him over to the Calligrapher because today is vaccination day for me. I finish at noon and make my way across town to the allocated venue. It is the parkade of a hospital and the queue winds all the way up three storeys of the parkade. At least it is breezy, and people are socially distancing.

A nurse comes to take my details. She has a checklist pinned to a clipboard.

'Have you been exposed to coronavirus in the past ten days?' she asks.

'Well, I work in the ED,' I reply.

'Obvious,' she beams, checks the yes, and moves on.

I finally arrive at the front of the queue. But it is just a decoy as, beyond the curtain, there are another two storeys of parkade. There are rows and rows of chairs and people are grouped and grouped again. We move from one batch of thirty chairs to another.

This goes on for three hours. Eventually we get to the actual needle, and it burns like a wasp sting. We all stand and move to the observation area. We must stay there for fifteen minutes, to check that we don't drop down dead or burst into flame. A buff paramedic sits down next to me, and we recognise each other from years in the ED.

'Are you pretending that it isn't sore? Or is it just my arm?' I ask.

'It is a bit sore,' he concedes. But he is wearing a mixed martial arts T-shirt so maybe he doesn't mind pain so much.

An official comes along to the observation area and tells us about all the possible side effects of the vaccine. I wonder why they did not do this before administering it, and I have a sneaky suspicion that I know the answer to that question.

Anyone knowing what could possibly go wrong would have turned around right at the bottom of the parkade. But then I think of the horrors of corona pneumonia, and what other option do I have? Even if I were to leave health care today, I would be crazy not to take the vaccine.

Damned if we do, damned if we don't.

Thirty

12 March 2021

The farm lies on a western slope, which provides the most beautiful afternoon light and sunsets full of intensity. But the sun is shy in the mornings; dawns are pale blue with the trees in their nightgowns on a carpet of shimmering dew.

I took today off today because I knew that I would feel rotten. All of my colleagues have warned me. I had a restless night and this morning it feels like there is lead in my blood.

I sit at the outside table with a mug of steaming coffee and a home-made rusk. Bliss, except for the fact that I have a fever of almost forty degrees and my skin feels hot and heavy. My stomach roils against the rusk, but I should have something to eat before I take the two paracetamol that I have set up on the table.

Interestingly, the face recognition software on my phone would not unlock my screen this morning. Maybe it knows that I have foreign protein in my blood.

I can see the golden paintwork of the sunrise on the opposite hill. The yellows and greens of the grass are washed with orange. We have yet to see the orb of sun, but the rays catch the rusty throats of the swallows overhead. It lends them fire as they dip and glide in the silent sky. A blue heron flies south to north, his wings beating deliberately and his legs trailing in the cool air beneath him. His neck folds back, and his glorious blue cap glitters.

I try to shake off a vague unease from a terrible dream that woke me at three in the morning.

Growing up, Easter was time for a pilgrimage to the sea. We would sit in the car for hours, watching the open land scroll by. Wild cosmos nodded and waved, whites and lilacs painting the grassland and yellow centres smiling at the sun.

In my dream we were making this journey, but it had a sinister foreboding.

We stopped at a picnic spot; a concrete table under a big tree somewhere near Warden. The dirt was hard, and the grassland drawn back, leaving plenty of room to pull off the ribbon of road. The cars swished by, their tyres whining and the wind buffeting as they passed.

There was a flask of coffee, lukewarm and too strong; hard boiled eggs and a tin of travel sweets. We tapped the eggs on the table to crack the shells and threw our litter in the barrel dustbin provided.

There was a particular smell about those picnics. Car upholstery, exhaust fumes and eggs. Also, the spicy wind from the open grasslands as the veld bobbed and parted in the wind.

Somehow, the very same scent was in my dream, mixed with the surgical spirits that they used to clean my arm for the vaccination and the gusty wind that blew through the parkade where we stood. There was a sense of a long, winding queue, and there were picnic tables with wolves behind the dustbins.

The car's wheels crunched along the gravel as we rejoined the tarmac to continue our journey to the coast. There was a fresh bite in the autumn air and fields of mielies, their leaves green and squeaky looking.

Closer to the sea, the maize gave way to sugarcane, and we craned our necks to get the first view of the deep blue ocean, nestled between the folded hills.

The wolves had followed us from the picnic spot, and they were streaking through the sugarcane, keeping pace with the car. I felt nauseous, but it was too dangerous to stop.

In the dream there were dead bears along the way, strewn like empty brown fur suits on the road. I swerved to avoid them, but we thumped over a good few. Then a huge oncoming truck braked and the super link behind it jackknifed and came sideways into our lane. It took up the whole parkade. Somehow, I managed to stop the car and go into reverse. I careened backwards, the radiator and grill of the truck filling my vision and the eighteen chrome wheels screeching and grinding.

It was gaining on me as I twisted and turned down the parkade in reverse. I woke up drenched in sweat. All that I could hear was the rush of blood in my ears and distant music. I tossed off the sheet and sat up. Took another two paracetamol and kept reminding myself that it was only a dream.

I sleep fitfully throughout the day and at sunset I drag myself out of bed for a five-minute walk with the snoopies. I am back, ensconced, before nightfall.

I keep thinking that I did not need the vaccine and that I should not have had it. I have not trusted my body to do what it has been doing for the last year.

I feel like a traitor.

I toss and turn all night, my left shoulder burning so much that I cannot lie on it, and the sheets drenched beneath me.

The rain roars on the tin roof in the middle of the night and the candles cast looming snoopy shadows on the walls.

The power is still out in the morning and the dawn comes later each day. I have two paracetamols with my morning coffee. If I have a fever when I arrive at the hospital, they will not let me in.

At six in the morning, I am at my post.

Thirty-One

Numbers in the ED are picking up, like the sea breeze of an afternoon. All the cubicles are full, and I scoot around, balancing ten or more patients simultaneously, like a seal with balls on its nose. Aside from the first day, I have recovered well from the vaccination and have plunged into the trough between the second and third wave and started swimming.

A young man and his wife are brought through. She reports that her husband has a facial droop. I ask him to take off his mask and he looks at me vaguely. I think he might be hard of hearing, so I step closer and ask again. He still looks bemused.

'Is he confused?' I ask. 'Very,' she replies. 'Over the last month or so. He has epilepsy and I think the medication does not agree with him.'

'Is it a new medication?' I ask.

'No, but he only started it four months ago. Since then, he has not been himself.'

'So, he was a newly diagnosed epileptic four months ago?' I don't like the direction in which this consultation is going. New epilepsy in a middle-aged person with no history of a head injury is worrying. Much more worrying when accompanied by evolving confusion and a facial droop.

A proper neurologist can spend an hour examining a patient. Not only do they check all the motor and sensory components of the brain and the spinal cord, but they also check reflexes and do cognitive skills tests. My assessment in the ED is much briefer. It consists of a few commands, like 'show me your teeth', which tests quite a few things at the same time.

It assesses whether the patient can hear, understand and action a task. It also tests the facial nerve.

Describing the course of the facial nerve is a favourite medical school question. It follows a complicated route, as does the aptly named vagus nerve. 'Vagus' means 'to wander' in Latin, hence the words 'vagrant' and 'vagabond' and 'vague'.

I digress. This guy cannot show his teeth; the right side of his face is paralysed. He is really confused and can't answer the most routine questions. His right leg is weaker than his left. And when I ask him to hold his arms out, palms up, his right hand drifts towards the centre and the palm turns downwards.

Called palmar drift, it is a sure sign that there is something wrong with his brain.

I tell them that they need an MRI scan of his head.

It seems that he had a brain scan four months ago, when his epilepsy was diagnosed. I check it on the system, and it was normal.

Today's MRI is far from normal. He has a massive brain tumour, taking up half of the space inside his head. The rest of the brain is being pressed to the side and down his spinal column. How he is even conscious is a mystery to me.

It is bad news. I spend time with them while we wait for the neurosurgery consultation. The good news is that the neurosurgeon, who is a genius with his hands, thinks that the tumour is well-positioned for removal with a laser knife. It is probably aggressive, as it appeared so suddenly, but this may make it more susceptible to chemotherapy.

I am working the two-to-ten shift this afternoon. The Calligrapher has the long haul – the nine-to-ten shift. Those are eleven long hours in a busy ED. We are working away in happy unison when the shift administrator pops in. She tells us the doctor working the night shift, who is supposed to start at nine in the evening, has tested positive for Covid. She will not be able to make it.

It is seven in the evening; two hours before her shift.

The Calligrapher and I look at each other. He has been here since nine in the morning; I arrived at two. So, I should stay. The problem is that I start again at six tomorrow morning. I cannot work the day, the whole night, and the day again. Well, I probably could, and I certainly have before, but I don't want to.

We look at the timetable and call a few friends. The notice is too late, and we cannot find anyone.

I have an idea.

'If you go home now and come back at two in the morning to do those four hours, I will work until two and come back at six.'

The Calligrapher considers it but tells me that he would not want his wife to drive home at two in the morning.

'Well, you are in luck on two fronts, then,' I tell him. 'The first is that I am not your wife. And the second is that we are not playing the gender card here. You have been here since nine. Go, now, while you have a chance.'

He looks uncertain and asks me again if I am sure.

'Run, Chicken Pup,' I tell him, using my favourite nickname for him. 'Run for the door. Go now, go, while the waiting room is empty.'

I sound like an FBI agent initiating a raid, but I feel sad and a little lonely as his taillights fade. Luckily, there are loads of fresh patients streaming in to distract me. Just before midnight the numbers lull and I spread my books on the little desk. The last two hours will go quicker if I lose myself in a topic of my choice. There are always little nuances that I hold in the back of my mind to research when I have a chance.

The Calligrapher arrives half an hour early and walks me to my car. The night feels wet, it is so dark. Suburbia is a twinkling carpet spread below us, an autumn moon hanging high in the sky. The brisk breeze through my scrubs makes me shiver.

Home for a nightcap and a few hours' rest, and I will be back with the sunrise.

This job. There has to be an easier way to make a living.

Thirty-Two

25 March 2021

Finally, I get to try surfing. The experience is delayed by almost a year, but the waves roll into the shore and the smell of salt and kelp is intoxicating and clean.

A buff young man shows us the stance, first on a skateboard and then on a board on the sand. He is young enough to be our grandson and I see that he is regarding these two grey-haired biddies with a mixture of amusement and mild trepidation.

Alida and I get the idea of standing on the board easily and manage to coast along by the end of the first lesson. The exhausting part is getting out through the surf. The teaching boards are long and wide and cannot be ducked under a breaking wave. This leaves us with the option of throwing the board over the wave, if it is shallow enough to stand, or leaving the board and diving under the wave. The unattended board is tugged back by the leash as the froth rides towards the shore.

Grandson does a splendid job of towing us out each time and tells us to just hold on.

The waves roll over us and I cling to the board like a wrung-out bat. The thudding salt water and the effort of getting onto the board are taking their toll and, an hour in, I tell him that I am done for the day. Alida looks relieved and we sit on the boards and chat as we wait for our last wave.

I feel like a real surfer.

It is not as easy as it looks, and I learned early not to let the board get between my body and the breaking wave. Grandson floats around us, somehow keeping both boards under control. His ability to read the ocean is impressive.

'Ready?' Grandson asks as he turns my board towards the shore for the last wave of the day.

'Yep,' I say and feel him give me a little shove before the wave picks me up. I stand on the board and ride just in front of the crest. The water is shallow, and I see the sand swirl brown in the backwash.

The board does a little jig to the left, there is a slight pain in my left ankle, and I fall to the right. As I tuck my legs under me to find the beach, I feel my left foot wash in the wave. It moves loosely in the current, slightly separate from my leg, and I know instantly that there is something wrong.

A wave breaks over me from the back and the board scoots forward, snatching my right leg from under me. I grab the Velcro leash and pull it free before the board tows me out again. Alida passes me, standing on her board, and sees me roll in the surf. I cannot stand on my left leg. I lift it out of the lacy water and look at my ankle.

Expecting a gruesome deformity, I see none.

I crawl up the beach and Grandson retrieves the board. Alida looks at my ankle and I roll over onto my stomach. Soles to the sky, I ask her to squeeze my calves. She obliges and I ask her if my feet move. Grandson looks on with amazement as she squeezes the right and then the left.

He has no idea that I work in the ED and that I have been on the business end of this for longer than I care to remember.

'Your left foot does not move,' Alida reports.

I have ripped off my Achilles tendon. With one tiny sideways movement of a surfboard; how completely random is that?

What a complete pain and utter inconvenience. In the moment, I think of how appropriately it is named. Dipped in the river Styx to make him invincible, Achilles's only weakness was the spot that his mother held him by the back of his ankle.

Paris found that spot with an arrow, as the legend goes. I recall that various people have been known to hack their adversaries' Achilles tendons to immobilise them before coming back later to finish them off. I can attest to the efficacy of this manoeuvre, as I cannot walk at all. Pain is not the limiting factor; my leg simply does not work.

I struggle up the sand, mostly carried by Grandson and Alida, who are both head and shoulders taller than me. I do my bat imitation, suspended between them with my left toe ploughing an intermittent stripe in the beach sand behind me. Grandson deposits me in the car and Alida goes to pay for the lesson before we make our way to the nearest ultrasound department. A complete rupture of the tendon is confirmed, and we travel back to Johannesburg for the surgery.

So much for our week by the seaside.

Thirty-Three

9 April 2021

Six in the morning and I am at my post, this time with crutches and a moon boot. I am a novelty and the staff crowds around me, asking what happened. The notion of learning to surf, especially in middle age, seems lost on them. After a while, I change the story to one in which I was pursued by a Bengal tiger. Its saber-sharp teeth sliced the tendon in half.

This version enjoys an enthralled and satisfied reception.

Two weeks of swinging along on crutches has made my arms ropey, but my left leg is wasting away, and it throbs when dependent. I clean the rubbish bin with steriwipes and set it up as a footrest. Then I sterilise all the surfaces before bringing out my belongings. My work bag has spent two long weeks in the boot of my car, where it was stashed almost exactly a fortnight ago, when we left for the beach. Such a lovely memory, heading south from the hospital, the sun dropping behind the Drakensberg mountain range. It was a long drive, but the roar and scent of the ocean made it worth our while. The apartment was right on the beachfront, the luminescent waves folding softly and rushing the shore.

Ocean liners were matt hulks where the sea met the star-studded sky. An absence of light, they could have been land masses or ships; we knew that they were the latter.

The dark bay glittered, and the waves sighed in greeting. What better place to have a whiskey on the rocks, feet up on the balustrade, and fall asleep to the rhythm of the sea.

Sadly, we were only at the beach for one day before having to head for home.

Sitting at my post, I think about the nerve damage caused by the gunshot ten years ago. The bullet lodged halfway through my spinal cord, causing a Brown Sequard syndrome. Initially, because of the swelling, I was paralysed. But, after a while, the neurology settled exclusively into the tracts that were disrupted. Some fibres cross over at the bottom of the spinal cord, meaning that the functions that they carry will be lost on the side opposite to the injury.

My resident bullet resulted in paralysis on my right side, but loss of sensation on my left. Even though I have made enormous strides in recovery, it is possible that the underlying injury made me more vulnerable to a tendon tear.

Or maybe I should have taken my own advice and not started a new sport after the age of fifty.

I make my way along the corridor on crutches at a painfully slow pace; the files clamped under my arm. I must stand on one leg while examining customers, sometimes losing my balance, and having to stop short of grasping a handful of a patient's hair to regain my equilibrium.

The shift drags by and my foot aches more and more. By midday, I am convinced that there is something else wrong. I take my sorry self down to my friends in the x-ray department. I want them to have a quick look and reassure me that this is just a bit of inflammation.

The head of radiology takes it upon herself to check my leg with the ultrasound. She taps the screen and taps it again. 'There it is,' she mutters under her breath. 'And there. And there again.' In the murky half-light, I ask the inevitable.

'There what is?

'The clot,' she answers, matter-of-factly. 'You are way too good a clinician not to have known it was there.'

I hang my head. I took blood thinners for ten days after the surgery to avoid exactly this complication. But she is right; I knew it was there. In all these years, I have never requested any kind of imaging. Now I am here, scrubs rolled up and the probe roving my sad-looking calf and vessels within.

There is an intimacy in the dark room. The radiologist's face is illuminated by the blues and greys on her screen, and I can see the concern in her eyes. We have been colleagues for twenty years and, although we do not see each other socially, I consider her a close friend.

Usually, we make light of situations, teasing and laughing together. Her eyes are a merry blue and she has a razor-sharp wit. But today she is not joking about anything.

'Could be the vaccination,' she murmurs.

'Sorry?' I'm not sure that I heard her correctly.

'Well, you know rollout will be stopped tomorrow because of unusual clotting profiles showing up three weeks after vaccination?'

I am sure that I look completely blank. Maybe my Achilles tendon was a link to thirty years of networking and knowing what was going on at any given time. I have over three hundred medical colleagues on my mobile and am present on most of their groups. Although they are all on mute, the articles, opinions and links can keep me entertained for hours. Now I feel a bit lost.

'Hmmm,' I say, staring at the ceiling. Whatever the reason, a deep vein thrombosis is not a good thing.

I can look forward to being booked off for yet another ten days, sitting in a chair with my foot up. Patience is not my strong suit, and this will be a difficult time for me. In addition, I hate taking medication, but I start immediately on little pink blood thinners, which will continue for another six months. I can't even blow my nose or brush my teeth without the risk of bleeding to death.

It is such a drag.

Thirty-Four

26 April 2021

Winter is here.

There is an icy wind buffeting the windows and bending the trees in the garden. The sky is a paler blue and the lush green farmland has become a flat tan. It makes the hills look smaller and more uniform. The light has changed from gold to silver and there are plumes of smoke on the horizon where the winter fires have begun. Dry air gusts by, hollowing out my nose and making my ears ache.

The snoopies roll on the lawn, crunchy flakes of dry kikuyu sticking to their coats, mobile lamingtons in the garden. Soon there will be a silver layer of frost, thicker on the west side of the walls and trees. Hollows and slopes will take longer to warm but the snoopies will know where to find the first rays.

I lever myself into the car and fold the crutches on the passenger seat. Despite feeling ungainly, I am looking forward to being at work again.

The day passes painfully slowly. I glance in the mirror while washing my hands and see that my forehead is smeared with blood. I am halfway through my shift, and no one has made mention of this. Wetting a piece of tissue, I wipe it off. My cuticle is bleeding, and I am spotting blood everywhere.

The joys of blood thinners.

A trolley rattles in at midday, paramedics flushed from the midday heat. A soccer player is strapped in, his leg dangling from an obvious break. He is screaming from the pain and his girlfriend is grasping his hand and running alongside. The paramedic crew is junior, so they are not qualified to give drugs. This has not worked out so well for the soccer player.

There are two bones in the lower leg, and he has snapped them both. His kneecap faces the ceiling but his foot droops sideways to the outside of the stretcher. The break is open, meaning that the sharp edges of bone have torn through the skin from the inside. There are a few winter leaves and some dry grass in the wound. I lean my crutches against the door and take a hold on his foot. If I can keep it in alignment while they move him over, it will make him much more comfortable.

I balance on my good leg while they get ready to move him across. On three, they lift him on the sheet, and I keep his foot with him. His girlfriend scurries around the bed and accidentally kicks my crutches away. I watch in dismay as one goes under the bed and the other down the corridor. I am now stranded, standing on one leg, holding onto a soccer boot. I look around for help. I might as well wash the wound out and get the leg in a temporary cast while I am here.

Most certainly, being on crutches is making me bad tempered. The same team of paramedics keep arriving at the door with a stream of patients, as if they are drawing on a secret stash. I am tired and cold and not in the mood. To annoy me more, they keep bringing people who are under the care of doctors at other hospitals.

In theory, if the patient is unstable, the paramedics must take them to the nearest hospital. And clearly there is a limit to how far out of the area an ambulance can go, to take a patient to a doctor who knows them. There is a fine line, though, and this paramedic team is overstepping it. They roll in with patient after patient, all of whom are existing patients of specialists at other hospitals in Johannesburg.

The first two are unstable and so I accept them without question. Once I have improved what I can, I get hold of their specialists and start the logistically tedious process of transferring them.

The third patient manages to get dropped off and accepted by the sister while I am busy with the soccer player. By the time I discover patient number three, she is sitting in the bed and the paramedics are long gone. I am stuck with her.

But I catch them in the act with patient number four.

She is a lovely granny with soft eyes and deep laugh lines around her eyes. The rest of her face is covered with a mask, but I can see from her respiratory rate and effort that she is short of breath. We chat briefly in the corridor, and she tells me that her pulmonologist is at a neighbouring hospital. Keeping eye contact with her, I firmly place the rubber tip of my crutch in front of the stretcher wheel.

The paramedic gazes down at the obstruction with surprise. I jerk my head to the side.

'Office,' I say under my breath.

The two paramedics chew gum and stare at me while I explain that this granny is under the care of a pulmonologist, whose name and number is front and centre of her documentation. She is also only on a hospital plan, which means that she will have to pay out of her pocket to open a file here, just so that I can pick up the telephone and tell her doctor that she is short of breath. She will have to pay for an x-ray and any blood tests that we do, and after that, pay for another ambulance to transport her.

'We agree that she will need admission?' I ask.

The paramedic duo shrug in unison.

'I mean, look at her respiratory rate and her blood oxygen levels,' I prompt.

They eye me with increasing suspicion and edge towards the door. I am not letting them off the hook.

'Because, if we agree that she will need admission, then is it not much simpler to call the number right here,' I stab the file and dial the number on my mobile, 'and ask her doctor, to whom she is well known, whether she will accept the patient?'

The phone rings once and the pulmonologist answers. Fixing the paramedics with a ferocious glare, I tell the specialist sweetly about Granny. She puts me on hold for a minute while she finds out about bed availability and accepts the patient graciously.

I write the ward and bed number down on the file and slap it into the paramedic's hand.

'We cannot take her to the other hospital,' the paramedic tells me. 'You will have to call and book a transfer.'

I resist the impulse to spit in his ear.

'This lady is a person, not a piece of furniture that you get to drop off wherever it suits you. How would you like it if your grandmother was treated like this?' I can feel that I am winding myself up now. Leave it, I warn my inner demon.

'Bleh!' I add.

I go and spend ten minutes with Granny and buy her a lime milkshake. Partly because she is confused and fearful but mostly, if I am honest, to annoy the paramedic team and make them wait outside. I have called their head office and the brass agrees that the same team can take her across at no extra charge.

I cannot carry the milkshake, of course, as my hands are otherwise occupied with the crutches, but I make a plan to get it from the coffee shop to the ED. She snakes the straw under her oxygen mask and closes her eyes with pleasure. I pat her hand and wish her luck.

I suspect that she might have Covid. The third wave has arrived with a rush.

My next patient also has shortness of breath. She also has a swollen calf and an abnormal ECG and so I send her down for a doppler ultrasound of her leg. I am suspecting that she has a clot there and that it is breaking up and sending fragments, or emboli, into her lungs. I write on the request form to please do the doppler and, if there is a clot, to progress to a CT angiogram. If there is no clot, just a plain chest x-ray will suffice.

The ED is ridiculously busy, and I lose track of her for a few hours. When her blood test results print, however, I go in search of her. She is not in the x-ray department, nor in the coffee shop, nor back in the ED. I try the contact numbers on her file to no avail. Sighing, I hobble back down to x-rays. The stairs are a real challenge on crutches and the lift is not working.

The sonographer tells me that she did the doppler and confirmed a large clot. But they could not do the CT angiogram because that side of the department has been dedicated to Covid investigations. They told the patient to come back the following day once the rooms and machines had been deep-cleaned.

Fantastic. Now I have lost track of a patient who could drop dead from a pulmonary embolism at any moment. I start calling the next of kin on the file and eventually get the patient back into the unit.

She has brought her husband and son as backup, and they all look at me inquiringly as I come into the room.

'So, you have a clot in your leg,' I tell her. Tears well up in her eyes and her family looks stricken. 'Don't worry,' I reassure her. 'I also have a clot in my leg.' I am not sure why I share this with her, but she looks enormously relieved. 'We need to start you on a blood thinner immediately and then get the CT angiogram as soon as possible. But with the shortness of breath and ECG changes, I am almost one hundred per cent sure that there are fragments already going to your lungs.'

A discussion ensues and we agree that she will be admitted to the ward. I want to give an injectable blood thinner immediately and it is calculated as units per kilogram.

'How much do you weigh?' I ask casually. She is a bit overweight.

'I have no idea,' she answers quickly.

'Approximately?' I prompt. She shakes her head adamantly.

'Okay, well let's weigh you then,' I tell her, 'as the anticoagulant must be correctly calculated.'

'Is that really necessary?' She is clearly very reluctant, but I insist. I guide her down the corridor to the scale which stands at the entrance of the ED. Her husband and son follow along. Seeing the look of dismay on her face, I hold up my hand to stay their progress.

'Girls only,' I tell them, and whisk the patient onto the scale. She does weigh a bit more than she should but I resist the impulse to say anything, or even read the weight out loud. I do the calculation in my head and write the clot buster up as a stat dose.

Sometimes, discretion is the best medicine.

Thirty-Five

7 May 2021

Our adversary Covid is back on the take. I know this because of the numbers in the ED, but also because of a particular feeling on my tongue. I thought nothing of it during the first wave but noticed that it returned with the second wave. I concluded that it was neither imagined nor co-incidence.

Today, the taste is back. More like a strange sensation, but I find myself examining my tongue in the rear-view mirror.

Covid seems more infectious this time around, with a different looking x-ray and a changed clinical course. I still cannot figure out how people with such terrible pneumonia can have totally normal-sounding air entry when I listen to their chests.

Just over 300 000 people had been vaccinated before the rollout was stopped. It was gradually re-initiated but today I hear that it has been stopped again. No one seems to know what is going on. Our president has suspended the secretary general of the ANC. In return, the secretary general is trying to suspend the president. Here at the coal face, the Johannesburg General Hospital has fallen victim to an arson attack.

I am, in equal portions, exhausted and outraged.

I am at work early. Partly because I could not sleep, but mostly because I must avoid traffic at all costs. Driving a manual car with only one leg is hazardous to all. Just yesterday I stood on the brake rather than the clutch, which resulted in a very sudden stop for myself and all those following behind.

It's well before six and I plonk myself down with a cup of tea and a slice of toast. I have taken to an early breakfast with my blood thinner. There is no sign of the night shift doctor. The ED is quiet so maybe he is having a short nap.

I am setting out my equipment for the day when I hear a commotion outside the double doors. Car doors slamming and the sound of shouting. The unit manager comes to call me.

'This guy is bleeding,' she tells me simply, but with urgency in her voice. I get up to follow her, chewing a corner of toast behind my mask. There is a perfect line of blood-stained bare footprints down the hall. Strange, I think to myself. I wonder where his shoes are.

The unit manager has put him on the bed. His shirt is soaked with blood and his right hand is wrapped in a sodden cloth. Pulling on gloves, I try to put pressure on the wounds.

'What happened?' I ask.

'My son stabbed me,' he replies.

'With a knife?' I ask.

'Yes.' He clearly thinks that that is a stupid question. 'I have lost a lot of blood.'

'I can see that,' I try to reassure him. To be honest these wounds look pretty bad. I grip his wrist to stem the profuse bleeding which I suspect is coming from his ulnar artery. With my left hand I put pressure on the neck bleed and my elbow on his chest. I am now trapped in position and ask the unit manager to put up a drip and get a sister to do some vitals.

This man is looking very pale.

The sisters seem unperturbed, but I am worried about the number and depth of the stab wounds. I can see five on his face and neck, and at least two on his chest. Two fingers of his right hand are almost severed in a defense injury. If the victim had not raised his hand to protect himself, I am pretty sure that he would be dead.

When the blood pressure cuff eventually arrives, I am even more concerned. It tells me that his systolic blood pressure is forty millimetres of mercury.

'Where is the drip?' I call out. The patient can hear a note of alarm in my voice.

'What must I do?' he asks anxiously. 'I am feeling bad.'

'Try to relax,' I tell him. He is holding his arms out on either side like a hovercraft. The more tense he is, the more blood wells up out of the boat-shaped wound in his neck. At least it is not bubbly blood, which would mean that his airway had been punctured. I let go of his wrist for a few seconds to apply a tourniquet; then put a pack of gauze on his neck and tape it down as tightly as I can without impairing his ability to breathe.

I snatch the stethoscope from around my neck and listen to his chest. Air entry seems equal and good, which is a relief, meaning that the knife has probably not punctured a lung. I still don't have a drip and I dash out of the cubicle to find out what is going on. A junior nurse is approaching with a drip set for a baby, with a tiny yellow cannula and an administration set with tubing thinner than spaghetti. I ask her if she is aware that the patient is bleeding to death, and we need two big bore lines. They are both going to have to go in his left arm, as his right is out of action.

I site the drip while calling down to the x-ray department. We need an urgent CT angiogram to see which, if any, organs or vessels have been damaged by the knife. Before angiograms were so easily available, the ED doctor would have to stick her finger into the wounds and feel about. This is not the most reliable test and the clean lines of contrast on a scan are way more accurate. It is also much more pleasant for us both.

We slide him into the donut of the scanner, and I watch from outside the room. I take the five minutes respite to call the general surgeon to let him know that there is a pending problem It is still before seven and I can hear his family in the background. They are still getting ready for their day.

I wonder why this man's son decided to attack him. This was not a small squabble; this was a serious intention to do harm.

Miraculously, there is no damage to his organs or vessels. Aside from his hand, which will need extensive plastic surgery to salvage, he has made a very lucky escape.

When I return to the ED with the patient, his wife and son have arrived. His wife is completely freaked out, but his son stares blankly at the wall. He refuses to speak to anyone, and I give him the summary that he will be either going to hospital or to jail.

'I won't do it again, doctor,' he says.

'No, you won't,' I reply. 'Not on my watch, anyway. Do you understand what a disaster today could have been for you? How terrible would it have been if you had actually killed your father? Or if the person that you attacked laid charges? It would ruin your life. All of your lives.' I include his shell-shocked mother, whose clothes are covered in blood.

'I don't need to be in the hospital,' the son tells me.

'Hospital, and by that, I mean a lock-up psychiatric unit, or jail,' I repeat. 'Hospital will be a lot more pleasant.'

A long family conference ensues, and eventually I get the son sedated and transported to a sympathetic psychiatrist. I return to my desk with a cold slice of half-eaten toast and tea.

Jeepers, only a few hours into the day and I am exhausted.

'Excuse me, doctor,' I turn to see his wife at the door.

'Yes?' I ask. I am weary of this family drama by now, as I am sure she is. Her waking hours must have been hell since before dawn. Her shirt is on inside-out and her hair is stiff with blood.

'Could I have a sick note for today?'

'Sure,' I say.

In truth, I would like to give her a sick note for the rest of her life.

Thirty-Six

15 May 2021

The media keeps telling us that we are not in the third wave yet. I am not sure why the official numbers are not matching what we are seeing in the ED.

I am going for my first physiotherapy session today. The therapist seems bored. She twiddles my toes, literally, for ten minutes until I check that she is aware that the repair is on the other side. I would have thought that the ten-centimetre scar down the back of my calf may have been a clue.

Her expression changes momentarily from bored to flustered and then back to bored again.

Thirty minutes later I am back in the ED, thinking that the past hour was a resounding waste of time and money.

Luckily the chair in the doctor's office has wheels, so I push off with my good foot and coast from surface to surface, where I have parallel patients cooking. Working in a busy ED is a bit like being a chef. Multiple pots on the boil, keeping an eye on dozens of things at any one time. One pile of notes for patients in to get x-rays, one for pending bloods, a few telephones for making and receiving calls.

One, increasingly large, pile of those discharged. I guess a burned meal, or a dissatisfied restaurant customer, is a less severe consequence than death if I lose focus, but otherwise, the balancing act is similar.

I see a boy and his mother returning from x-rays. He was injured in a rugby scrum and has a painful shoulder. He is only seven and as scrawny as a bird. I cannot feel anything broken on examination but have sent him for imaging. His mother is like a painted doll, with a bright red mouth that is constantly settled in a surprised little 'o'. She is almost flirtatious with her son, covering her eyes and mouth and saying 'you are so brave' repeatedly.

I go to tell them that the x-ray is normal and give him a sling and some painkillers.

'Doctor,' Mom asks, smoothing her hair. 'When will he be able to play again?'

'Probably not for a week to ten days,' I tell her, 'depending on how it feels.'

'He has a big match tomorrow,' she tells me.

I can see his eyes grow large behind his mask. 'I won't be able to play tomorrow,' he says immediately.

'It is really important. Team selection,' Mom adds and looks at me. 'You are so brave,' she adds over her shoulder and dabs the corner of her eye.

Pure steel, this lady.

'Definitely not tomorrow,' I say.

'Let's see how he feels, poor darling,' she concludes and sweeps him away. One hand between his prominent shoulder blades, she propels him towards the door. He glances back at me and my heart sinks for him. It must be tough, trying to live a lie.

Perhaps he will become wary and never completely present. Some families are good at secrets, but they wear you down, making you a stranger to yourself. He will probably learn to craft his answers and keep up a pretense. After layer upon layer, I think that he will lose sight of himself entirely.

It is depressing.

The ED is mayhem today. Usually we see a couple of 'priority one' patients per day – patients who are in imminent danger and must be attended to within minutes of their arrival. Today, I have had ten 'priority one' patients in the last six hours. None of them have Covid, as far as we know, so they are taking up all ten non-Covid beds in the unit. Because all of them have true emergencies, they should each have their own nurse. This is wishful thinking, because there are only five nurses on shift.

Actually there are only four, because one has locked herself in the bathroom and refuses to come out unless I write her a note saying that she does not have to nurse patients with Covid pneumonia.

I am also concerned that this new variant of Covid is not showing up on the tests. Both the rapid antigen test and the formal PCR seem increasingly unreliable.

To add to my difficulties, the cardiac catheterisation laboratory has had to close unexpectedly. This presents a huge challenge as our hospital is known as one of the top centres for acute management of heart attacks. I am trying to get a message through to the paramedic services not to bring possible heart attacks to us. Called 'putting a unit on divert', this used to be as simple as making a call to the person in charge. But medicine, like most things, has become increasingly political. To get a unit on divert means jumping through a whole heap of hoops. And I don't have time for hoops while I try to save people from dying without the benefit of opening their vessels and reperfusing the heart muscle. This is what we used to do in the old days, and what hospitals without the benefit of the catheterisation lab do every day.

I don't like it at all. It is difficult, and very stressfull for the team to cope without what has become an essential part of programme.

By the time I get home, I am exhausted. The snoopies are waiting in the dark; they have already been dressed for bed. Their thick rugs have an extra strap to ensure that they do not slip off, which is especially useful for evening jaunts. We had leftover satin ribbon, so the coats are fastened with a neat bow on the left side. This means that every morning is like unwrapping Christmas gifts:

a smooth tug of the shiny ribbon and the coat falls away, revealing the toasty snoopy beneath.

They all line up to greet me, their long noses as cold as the night. We have a stroll around the garden to stretch our legs. Greyhounds are tall dogs, and their silky ears are perfectly placed for patting.

There is no moon, and the constellation Orion is cartwheeling on the eastern horizon. The three jewels of his belt are so bright I can almost pluck them down; his shoulders and legs are twinkling points, and even his scabbard is a smattering of stars. He is a hunter, but tonight I cannot see his bow and shield. Orion is one of the few constellations visible from both hemispheres and is so familiar in the inky sky.

We are taking a pounding from Covid, and I wish that I could hide away here on the farm until it is over. I am not sure, though, whether it will ever be over. It seems to be getting more contagious and increasingly deadly.

Alida has made a roaring fire and we watch the flames crackle and dance until the day recedes. I have not touched my cello or piano for over a year, and I wonder where the music has gone.

Thirty-Seven

22 May 2021

Dealing with complaints is probably the second worst part of my job. It ranks close on the heels of breaking bad news. Responding to complaints is usually the task of the most senior doctor in the unit. Sometimes the patients or families are completely correct in their criticism, in which case I am happy to organise refunds and initiate training to prevent a recurrence. But every now and then a complaint comes along that is just stupid or malicious; these ones are such a waste of time and energy.

Today is one of those days.

I am given a telephone number and told to call this patient back. He wants to speak to the person in charge.

I look around the unit, which looks like a battlefield in mid-fight, and wonder who is in charge. It certainly doesn't feel like me.

I retrieve his file and see that he was seen last night by a very competent doctor. I call the number. I can hear from his tone that he is furious.

'I was seen last night, and I am very unhappy with the service. I want a refund.'

'What is it that you are unhappy about?' I ask.

'Well, first of all, I waited three hours.' I check the time on the stickers, the nursing notes, and the doctor's notes. The patient is clocked at each stop, so I can tell that he did not wait at all.

'And then I got a drip and blood tests and was sent down for x-rays. All of the results were normal, so now I have this account for over R3000, and I am not on medical aid and none of this was necessary.'

I look through the notes and tell him that the nurse in triage documented that he was complaining of lower abdominal pain and lay down on the floor in the waiting room. He was brought through as a priority one patient. He was rolling around on the examination room floor too, as documented by the doctor, and so they put up a drip with pain medication. I think that a drip is justified in any patient who takes to the floor in agony. And if his abdominal pain was so bad, he definitely needed blood tests and an x-ray.

So far, his chances of a refund are pretty small.

I tell him, further, that we do not treat patients differently according to their financial means. I give him an example.

'If a patient has chest pain, we must do an ECG, whether or not they are on medical aid.'

'So why didn't they do an ECG on me then?'

There is a moment of silence, while I wonder whether this guy is for real.

'Um, because you had pain in your lower abdomen, not in your chest,' I answer. 'An ECG would have been an unnecessary expense.'

'So, what was wrong with me, then?' he asks, changing tack.

'I did not see you,' I remind him, 'so I can only go on the notes and the results of the tests. Which were all normal. Are you still having pain? Because I am happy to reassess you free of charge.'

'No, the pain has gone away. But with all the costs incurred, I want some answers.'

'We often do tests in order to exclude things, and having a clear negative result is a good thing,' I try to explain.

'Well, I am not paying this account.' He has a finality in his voice, and I conclude that the conversation is over from my side, too.

'OK, well I am sure someone from the hospital accounts section will deal with that, going forward,' I tell him. 'And I am glad that the pain is resolved.' He did not hear the last part, because he had already hung up.

I should send him an account for a follow-up consultation, I think to myself. Instead, I go and make tea and peer through the curtains at the Covid section. All the beds are full in there, with monitors chiming and nurses looming large in PPE.

We are swimming and swimming, but we don't know which way is up.

I must remember to stop at the shop to get groceries on the way home. I tear off a sheet of script paper to make a quick list. I jot down some spices, butternut and onions.

The unit manager comes to tell me that there is a new patient waiting.

'OK, OK thanks, Onion,' I say absently. 'Be there in a minute.'

There is a small stutter in her gait, and she turns back to me. 'Did you just call me onion?' she asks.

'Did I?' I look up over my glasses. I wouldn't put it past me. I am so distracted; I finished my conversation just the other day with an unknown colleague by signing off with 'love you.' He was as startled by this, I am sure, as the unit manager is to be referred to as an onion. I show her my grocery list and we both have a giggle.

Crazy times like this, we have to laugh or cry. One thing I know is that we cannot carry on like this. The new variant is a curveball, pitched to a team that is too tired to care. I wonder what we can do to recover ourselves.

I am so tired of seeing people who are starving for oxygen; tired of trying to explain what I cannot understand. Each new case that comes through our doors, I must ask myself whether we have the resources to treat this person and when we are all going to get this violent variant.

For the second time in the space of a year, my relationship with medicine seems precarious. And there is not even surfing to look forward to.

I hear a patient telling the sister in triage that he must come straight through, as he is having a heart attack. I adjust my chair on wheels so that I can see the front desk. He looks about twenty, but the sister brings him through anyway.

'I am having a heart attack, doctor,' he tells me earnestly.

'Really?' I ask. 'How do you know?'

'Well, it is the same pain as my last heart attack.'

'Really?' I ask again. 'And when was that?'

'Last year,' he tells me.

'Mmmm hmmm,' I am leaning against the wall. 'And then what happened?'

'I was admitted to the cath lab for a stent.'

In the space of those few words, my demeanor changes from nonchalant to attentive. If he knows the words, he's done the dance. I motion the sister over for an urgent ECG.

In the next cubicle a little girl screams non-stop. She was bitten by a rabbit at the bunny park and the very tip of her finger is gone. The finger is being soaked in saline before we dress it.

In an unprovoked attack by a wild animal, one must always consider rabies. I think this case is very low risk, but the mother of the bunny victim is beside herself with concern. She had read up and insisted on the full course of prevention. Luckily, this is not a decision made by the ED doctor. The immunoglobulins to fight rabies are in short supply and therefore are controlled by the National Institute of Communicable Diseases. The NICD has a four-page form for the ED to complete, and they make the decisions from there.

As I suspected, a rabbit kept in a bunny park does not qualify as a wild animal. I also doubt that the attack was unprovoked, but I know better than to open that avenue of enquiry. Bad enough that I had to break the news to the mum that the little fragment, which she had somehow managed to wrest from the attacking bunny, would not be able to be re-attached.

The last patient for whom I insisted on a full course of rabies prevention had been the victim of a bat attack. He was lying on a lounger, sunbathing, when a bat flew down out of the blue and bit him on the thigh. He swatted the bat with his flip-flop and came to the ED, cradling the corpse. The local vet ran an urgent test for us, and it came back a definite positive.

Many patients bring demised scorpions, spiders or snakes as evidence of the bite. One rural family even brought a python that had swallowed a small child. There was not much for me to offer on that one, but it stands out in my memory as one of the most awful and out-of-the-ordinary consults of my career.

Thirty-Eight

15 June 2021

The third wave is much worse than the first and second combined and we are not coping at all. There are no beds available anywhere and the patients keep rolling in. We don't know where to put them and tempers are short. Paramedics, nurses, doctors and administrators are cornered and desperate and the friction between us is increasing.

I can see that a policy decision has been taken by the hospitals that they cannot close their doors to patients. I understand and appreciate this, but the hitch in the system is that there is only so much space on the front line. If we cannot keep the flow of patients moving from the cars and ambulances into the wards, then everything backs up. It is like water attenuation, or a massive highway closure with traffic from hell. The ED is full, and the ambulances wait in the bays to offload. Members of the public cannot get ambulance transport, so twice as many people are coming in by car. Many tell us that they are Covid positive on arrival, which is also a novelty.

We are now obliged to keep these 'known positives' separate from all the other coughing, feverish people who are also probably Covid positive but just don't know it yet. Family and friends of patients in the car park make desperate attempts to get through the double doors of the ED and request help. We do not have portable oxygen to take out into the carpark, although I hear that some will be delivered this week.

For now, we have oxygen concentrators. But they need to be plugged in and we don't have an extension cord. Alida brings us two from the farm, but the cars must be close to the window where our cables loop out, a lifeline to the patients. It adds an extra layer of chaos, these cars parked at awkward angles to the doors and windows of the ED, and it makes ambulance access impossible.

I must keep reminding myself that they could be my family, and I would want help for them.

All that I want to do is hide in a cupboard until the end of my shift and then make it someone else's problem.

The divide between private health care and the government service widens by the day. In years gone by, if an unstable patient without any funding arrived in the private ED, our mandate was clear. Stabilise as best we can and then call the local government hospital to transfer out. Sometimes we would get a bit of a run-around, but with some determination we always squeezed them in somewhere.

This is no longer the case.

Once the patient is allocated a bed in a private facility, the government hospitals, filled beyond breaking point, decline to take them. They are either too busy to pick up the telephone when we call or else they tell us straight out that they are full. I have taken to warning patients about the situation, but no one wants to listen. Despite my explanation of how the system works, and that those desparate for a bed must choose a 'stream' at the outset – government or private – and stick with it, patients are too frightened to listen.

I am exhausted with trying, and and I cannot make it my problem. I do my job: see the patients, do the investigations and write the notes. Then I give the file to the sisters and tell them that the patient needs to be admitted. They give the file back and tell me that there are no beds. I let the file rest on the corner of my desk. They pile up. I am on every ED network in Johannesburg. I know that there are no beds anywhere. All that I can do is put their name on the Joint Operations Committee and wait. Now the patients are blocking the beds and I just keep adding files to the pile. I propose that we get a dedicated in-tray for patients awaiting beds. The unit manager looks at me like I am a complete lunatic. I shrug and busy myself writing reams of medications for the patients who are lucky enough to score a bed.

It is eventually dawning on us that we are going to have to fly these patients out of Johannesburg to secure ICU beds in other major provinces and cities.

The red phone rings and rings. I eventually answer it and the paramedic tells me that they are bringing a priority one patient with Covid pneumonia. I tell them that there are no beds on which to resuscitate the patient. In any case, the doorbell chimes five minutes later. I am closest, so I answer the door. I am faced with the paramedic who called a few minutes ago on the emergency line. I look at him over my mask and feel annoyance creep up.

He opens with 'We have a P1 patient with Covid.'

'Yes. You called. We have no beds in the unit,' I counter. I want to add, 'same as five minutes ago,' but I don't.

'So, you are refusing to accept the patient?' The paramedic is obviously at the end of his tether.

Sadly, so am I.

'At this time, we have no beds in the unit. You can choose to wait in the ambulance bay or call around to find bed availability.'

'I want to speak to the unit manager,' he says, rudely brushing by me. But the battle lines are drawn, and I follow him into the unit manager's office. After he has a rant about how hospitals are not allowed to turn patients away, she assures him that I am correct that there are no beds and that we will bring the patient in when we can, he turns to leave.

I am blocking the doorway, leaning on the frame with my arms crossed. I am not tall in stature, but the look in my eyes brings him to a halt.

'So, I'm just checking here. You are wearing full PPE and have just come out of the back of an enclosed space, where you have spent significant time with a known Covid patient in respiratory distress, and yet you find it appropriate to come in here, without even washing your hands, walk through the entire ED and then into the office of the unit manager, who happens to be over sixty years of age with other risks. Does that seem right?'

I know that I am being argumentative, but I can't seem help it. He stares at me, and I can see him clocking me as 'one of those doctors'.

But I am on a roll. 'And I see that this is a private patient. So, I hope that you have counselled them correctly before bringing her to us, rather than a government facility. Because, the way it is at present, there are no transfers available. State will only see the long line of people in their own queues. There are no shortcuts to getting in via a private casualty.'

'I told them.' He is surly, at best.

'You told them a few hundred thousand rand?' I push the issue.

'Not my business to give quotes.' He is now openly belligerent.

I shrug and walk away, leaving him to the unit manager, who is also gazing at me in consternation. This show of temper is very unusual for me, but I am totally fed up with this pandemic and the pressure on us to solve everything. While people still go out for lunch and the schools stay open, the virus spools out and we must try and stop a flood with a mop.

If I had it in my heart to quit, now would be the time.

But I don't. I just change my mask and gloves and press on. There is this intransigence; a doggedness in my heart that still holds fast. I can't tell if it is stupidity or bravery – sometimes the borders between the two become blurred. I hear a voice telling me to put up my dukes and fight. Asking if I'm a coward. Asking if I am beaten. My answer is clearly no, and I add a wry 'not yet' with a little smile.

The voice is so real that it halts me for a moment, and I glance behind me. My mother has been dead for almost 40 years. I could not conjure her voice nor image if I tried.

The paramedics get their way and I see them wheeling their patient into the next available bed. Never mind the ten people in the waiting room. I go and see her immediately so that I can assess the problem. Her son, accompanying her, looks like a rapper, with heavy gold chains and trousers hanging low. L'il Rapper, I think, maybe he has loads of cash.

Her oxygen saturation is low, despite a high flow mask. She has risk factors, including diabetes, blood pressure and obesity. Before we do a chest x-ray or blood tests, I can tell she will need admission. I fill in the forms and ask the sister to start looking for a bed.

'She is a private patient, doctor,' the sister tells me immediately. I am so over all of this, I simply tell her that I know that; I have explained the situation to the family via the paramedics and they have chosen private care. There is not much I can do about this; she is here now and so we must see her.

The administrator at the front desk asks the family for the cash. Of course, they do not have any cash at all. I suggest that they go outside and catch the paramedics before they leave and ask them to take them to the government hospital down the road.

As is always the case in these situations, the paramedic refuses outright to help them. His job was to take the patient from home to the hospital. He is not now going to reload her and travel the city looking for another hospital. He has successfully made his problem mine. And, in true pandemic adaption mode, I am handing the problem straight to the family. Unless they expect me to give them the cash, there is not much that I can do to change the situation. I cannot adjust the cost estimate or the fact that his mother needs admission.

L'il Rapper comes to the doctors' office to find me. He bumps me with his elbow in greeting.

'Yo. Don't have that kind of cash. Can you lend me your car to take her to the other hospital?' he asks.

'Excuse me?' I am not sure that I heard him correctly.

'I don't have transport,' he explains. 'And I blew my last bacon on the ambulance to come here.'

There are so many things wrong with this scenario. Clearly the paramedic did not speak to the patient about taking them to the appropriate facility. Secondly, there is no way I would lend my car to some unknown person under most circumstances, even to L'il Rapper, whose care for his mum is so desperately clear.

The unit manager comes to look for me. Her eyes are worried above her mask.

'I need you,' she says simply.

'Excuse me,' I say to L'il Rapper. 'Gotta go.' I resist the impulse to do a little jig and bump his gold-ringed knuckles as I depart.

I scoot around the corner into the Covid resuscitation room. A massive man is sitting on the bed, his arms in tripod position, bracing himself to keep breathing. Sweat is pouring off his face and his skin is grey. The monitor tells me that his oxygen saturation is 42% despite the highest flow oxygen mask that we have.

He is in trouble. And, by association, so are we. Because there are no ventilators in the hospital. Grim has got this guy for sure, unless I can pull a rabbit out of a hat. Right at the beginning of the pandemic, I watched a podcast from the chaos in Italy and Spain where the patients were piling up in the corridors and boardrooms. They used an anaesthetic machine to ventilate some patients in times of crisis.

I know where the anaesthetic machines are and elective surgery is closed at the hospital, so I could use one. Theoretically. The truth is that I don't know how to use those specific machines, but I guess that I am going to find out pretty soon.

I tell the gasping patient to hold on and run to the theatre complex, speed-dialing the matron as I go to ask permission. She gives it the thumbs up, if we make sure to use filters and clean the machine as soon as we can change to a conventional ventilator.

My next message is an urgent plea for help. 'Any anaesthetists at or near the hospital?' I type on our emergency hospital group.

My phone pings a reply as I unplug the closest machine and trot back to the ED. Mountain Man is still gasping. I look at the group and see three anaesthetists are in the area, but none are currently available. As I scroll through the message, my phone rings. It is one of my colleagues, an anaesthetist who is always ready to help. He cannot come in, but he will talk me through how to set up the machine.

What I need is high pressure ventilation and that is not the default setting for giving an anaesthetic. A bit like taking an aeroplane off autopilot, I must change all the settings and then flip a switch to confirm that I am in charge.

'There is a blue button at the bottom of the screen, second from the left,' he tells me. 'Click on it, then scroll to the following option.' And so we go, changing the settings until we are ready to run.

I put my hand over the end of the tubing to check if I can feel the pressure. Nothing. Mountain Man is so desperate that he tries to put his nose in my hand, nudging his way to the oxygen flow.

'Hold on just a few more seconds,' I tell him. He is not coping on high flow oxygen by mask; there is no margin for error in the changeover.

'It's not working,' I tell the anaesthetist. I can feel him close his eyes on the other side of the phone, visualising the machine in front of him.

'The green switch!' he says suddenly.

Of course! The green switch is hidden away, purposefully, so that it doesn't get flipped by mistake. It tells the machine to do my bidding, even though the parameters are unusual. I clunk it over and, voila, I can inflate ten balloons at once. The pressure hisses out and Mountain Man is saved.

I sense Grim slinking out of the cubicle. I feel an enormous sense of victory; I'm rocking this machine like a professor.

Perhaps L'il Rapper has rubbed off on me.

Thirty-Nine

4 July 2021

I am working in a war. We have given up any pretense of normality. I have a headache and a sore throat, but I think that it is more exhaustion than Covid. At least, I am hoping so. Alida has managed to have her first vaccine, which is an enormous relief. I would never forgive myself if I made her sick and I can't figure out whether the virus can travel on my skin or hair even if I sanitise myself from head to toe.

Research is showing that this massive surge is probably due to the Delta variant of the virus. Originating in India, it is a hundred times more contagious than our home-grown South African Beta variant. It also makes people sicker for longer, which is really creating a bottleneck at the hospital.

I have started just admitting patients on how they look from the door. Any excess respiratory effort, and I get out my mobile to photograph their name and put them on the list waiting for beds. I am filling up beds as fast as they empty; and, sadly, they are not emptying because of patients being discharged.

I should think that the undertakers are doing very brisk business. It must be horrible, to share a ward with someone and watch the doctors and nurses running in to try and resuscitate them. So far, CPR on patients with Covid pneumonia is zero per cent effective.

We have not managed to get one back from Grim; once their heart stops from Covid pneumonia, it is game over.

This is expected, as a resuscitation can only be successful if we can find and address a reversible cause. Hence the Hs and Ts that the resuscitation professors buzz around continuously. If you can find the reason that the heart stopped, and remedy that, you have some chance of making a save from Grim.

Covid pneumonia, with its associated lung clots and heart problems, is not something that we can solve in three or four minutes while we hold the fort with CPR. When we are on the clock with it, Grim wins hands down every time.

And there is a large, red clock above the resuscitation beds in almost all EDs. When you start CPR, the timekeeper presses the start button. They then call out each minute that passes, what we have done, and what must be done in the next minute. This adds an extra layer of chaos but is very useful if you lose your place.

If you happen to be doing a resuscitation somewhere other than your own unit, you can download an app to keep time and remind you of the next step.

After five unsuccessful resuscitations and having to break the bad news to five desperate families, I am feeling deeply contaminated. I decide to have a shower – at least we still have hot water and towels and fresh scrubs.

A sister calls me to a patient. His main complaint is that he feels dizzy and lightheaded. He is young man, a bit overweight, with glowing green eyes. He reminds me of the Cheshire Cat. Not that I have ever met a Cheshire Cat, but anyway, I have an idea of how they should look.

Cheshire has no other medical history, but he is stressed out because his wife died from Covid last week. He feels anxious and generally unwell. I glance at his temperature and oxygen saturation on the front of his file. They are both normal, so there is no obvious sign of the germ. But his heart rate is high – 145 – so there is something cooking. I ask the sister to do blood tests, an ECG and give him a mild sedative.

Maybe he is just anxious.

When I come back to check on Cheshire, he is sound asleep in the bed. His heart rate is now 160. I stare at the ECG; it looks like a fast but normal rhythm. There is, of course, an algorithm to follow. When I coach younger doctors, I try to simplify things. I ask them first whether the heart rate is too fast or too slow. Then I ask them if the patient is stable or unstable. Each answer leads to a different path.

I would do well to heed my own lessons.

Cheshire is going too fast, and he is stable. I wake him up to ask him a few more questions.

His reply to all my enquiries is negative. No pain, no bleeding, no gastro-intestinal symptoms, no chest pain. Nothing except feeling light-headed. I do another ECG and get the ultrasound machine to check for any free fluid in his abdomen. It would be very unusual if he had ruptured an organ or vessel with no history of trauma and no pain, but I have a nagging feeling that his pulse is fast because he is trying to compensate for something. Something like blood loss, says the little voice in the back of my head; or maybe infection, except that he does not have a temperature.

Bleeding, the little voice says.

I am standing at the bed, my brain doing a searching inventory, when Cheshire tells me that he is feeling worse. A faint sheen of sweat coats his brow.

I tell the younger doctors that, when any patient starts to sweat, so should we.

I push the button to recheck his blood pressure and I see that it is dropping. His pulse is faster, 180 now, and I must act. My team is ready with the drug I need; a chemical to stop his heart for a few seconds in the hope that it starts again in a normal rhythm. It is hair-raising for all, especially the patient, but I tend not to tell them that I am planning on stopping their heart. I just tell them that this medication is going to make them feel really weird for 30 seconds or so.

I stop Cheshire's heart twice, but it goes straight back up to 180. By now the cardiologist has arrived and he hovers behind me, watching the rhythm strip spool out of the machine.

'Sinus tachycardia,' he says, confirming my suspicion that this is a compensation for something else.

'What does that mean, doctor?' Cheshire asks. His eyes are glowing even greener.

'It means that your heart is beating too fast, but I am not sure if that is because there is an underlying problem, like bleeding, that it is trying to make up for, or if the primary problem is your heart. Are you absolutely sure you have not passed any blood in vomit, urine or stool?' Cheshire shakes his head adamantly.

He is also sure that he does not want any more of the drug that we gave him.

'It felt like my heart stopped, doctor,' he tells me earnestly. Funny you should mention that, I think to myself. 'And who is this other man?' Cheshire enquires.

'Oh, um, this is the cardiologist,' I say, introducing them. 'I got him specially for you,' I add, with a wink.

'Oh, thank you.'

Cheshire is such a polite guy. I wish I knew what was wrong with him.

I decide not to try and intervene with his heart again but rather to run in fluids and get some second opinions. The cardiologist is pretty sure that this is nothing to do with his heart but suggests a small dose of a drug called a calcium channel blocker to try and slow him down. I write it up and the sister gives it.

It makes no difference.

At last, I hear the printer click and whir. I snatch up Cheshire's blood results and, finally, I have a clue. A kidney function test is one of the basics that we run. Blood levels of urea, which is excreted by the kidney, increases if the kidneys are not working properly or if the patient is dehydrated. A lesser-known fact is that, when blood is present in the gut, it is reabsorbed as urea. An isolated high urea in a young guy with no reason to be dehydrated might very well mean a bleed into his stomach or colon.

Cheshire might have an active bleed in his duodenum, which is between his stomach and his colon. If the blood was in the stomach, he would have vomited it up. Blood is an irritant to the stomach lining and gets chucked quickly. A bleed into the colon makes its way into the stool within a few hours. But the duodenum, with its excellent blood supply and surprising lack of symptoms, is a dangerous area.

The Professor used to point out the duodenum and pancreas and warn me, in dulcet tones, that these were tiger country. It always made me smile, as there are no tigers in Africa, but I looked out for them anyway as we stared over the green drapes and into the surgical field.

I ring the surgeon on call and ask him to take the patient for a gastroscope. He asks what symptoms Cheshire has. I tell him a raised blood urea and an unexplained fast heart rate.

'So, why does he have to have an urgent scope?'

'Because even though his haemoglobin is holding and his blood pressure has improved with fluids, I think he has a big bleed.'

The surgeon sighs. I have him cornered, though, and it is just a matter of time. I keep silent until he sighs again and says 'OK, admit him under me.'

Later that afternoon he sends me a picture of the inside of Cheshire's duodenum. The whole thing is a massive ulcer, spurting blood furiously. Cheshire almost bled out and they had to resuscitate him on the table.

'What a fantastic save from Grim!' I congratulate the surgeon.

'Well, you called it,' he answers. 'At least you didn't give him a calcium channel blocker. That would have killed him for sure.'

'Ah, well,' I hesitate and then decide on full disclosure. 'I actually did. But it was a very small dose…' I tail off.

Jeepers. Cheshire and I dodged a serious bullet there. I stopped the guy's heart – not once but *twice* – while he was bleeding out.

His heart was desperately trying to make up for the decreased volume of blood in the system and I was trying to slow it down or, even worse, stop it completely.

That is the problem with protocols, though. The protocol for a very fast, and therefore inefficient, heart rate is to cardiovert, or stop the heart, and hope it will start again in a regular rhythm. While Cheshire was stable, I had time to think. But once he became unstable, I had to act. How would it look, in retrospect, that his heart went faster and faster until it stopped, and I had just stood about watching?

I go out to the shirking wall and get some sun on my skin. I am deeply grateful that I managed to get one on the board against Grim, especially a nice guy like Cheshire.

A car swoops into the parking lot and a guy hobbles out of it with a tea towel wrapped around his lower leg. A customer; might as well get him seen. I go in through the back door and meet him in the triage room. I unwrap his leg and the blood wells up. I press on it with the tea towel and ask the sister for a stitch tray. The wound is about ten centimetres long and very deep.

'Are you sure it needs stitches, Doc?'

'Yep. For sure.' I tell him. 'How did you cut it?'

'I was scratching my leg with a knife. I was slicing the Sunday roast and my leg got, like, really itchy.' I glance up at him.

'Seriously?' I ask.

'Yeah. Didn't know it was so sharp.'

'Funny thing about knives,' I say. 'Unexpected sharpness.' He seems the kind of guy that I can joke with.

'Yeah,' he says, seriously. 'Maybe I should press less hard next time. It was very itchy though.' He stares balefully down at the massive swathe of gaping skin.

'Maybe try a butter knife rather,' I suggest, as I tie the first of many little nylon knots. When I am done, it looks like he has been bitten by a great white shark.

Impressive handiwork, even if I say so myself.

Forty

8 July 2021

Today, two unexpected things happened.

Firstly, Jacob Zuma was sentenced to fifteen months in prison for contempt of court. It is the first big step for our troubled country out of the dismal mess that we have made, and I feel remotely hopeful.

The second thing is that I have Covid.

It had to happen, eventually. I really was beginning to feel like I was bullet-proof.

I played a lot of sport on the weekend and my body was aching. As a child, Saturdays were spent running wild. Riding ponies, walking to the shops, running to our friends and riding more ponies. There was no thought of drinking water or applying sunscreen and I used to arrive home exhausted and dehydrated. I would lie on the floor near the bathroom tap and glug down as much as I could.

Despite a hot bath, I was feeling the same this past Sunday night. My bones ached; my hair ached. I was roasting hot then freezing cold. I have had a nagging sinus headache for a few days. This morning I have a runny nose and a slightly scratchy throat. I pull my mask up firmly and keep seeing patients. It is probably just a cold and, anyway, all the patients have Covid. I need not worry about infecting them.

But the unit manager is too switched on for me.

'Are you sick?' she asks, fixing me with an eagle eye.

'Mmmm. Scratchy throat,' I reply. 'Nothing to worry about.'

'We must swab you.' Her radar for Covid has become laser sharp.

'OK,' I say half-heartedly. Only half an hour of my shift left anyway. I hope that she forgets. But no, she is waiting with the test in hand as I come out of the next consultation.

The stripes show up so fast and heavy that even I am surprised. She shakes her head and says, 'Sorry.'

I pack my things and wait in the car for the next doctor to arrive. I hand over to him by telephone when I see his car enter the parking lot.

It feels weird, to be sent home without so much as a word to anyone.

The weirder thing is that I don't want to tell anyone. I call Alida immediately and have an awkward conversation about one of us moving out. She has tested positive but that was more than a year ago and she had minimal symptoms. With the new variants and the extremely high viral load in Gauteng, I don't think that she is safe. I have probably exposed her already, though, and we talk through the implications.

The next call is to my friend and neighbour. We walk our dogs together most evenings and she visits the farmhouse for a glass of red. Luckily, I have only seen her twice in the past week; but still, she needs to know. She sounds disheartened by the news.

Calls to my brother and a few other dear friends, and I slink off to lick my wounds.

It is a long ten days. A beastly headache hounds me, and the fever comes back every afternoon. By dusk, I find myself in layers of jerseys and dressing gowns, hunkered next to the fire. There are snoopies strewn everywhere, with Pookie hogging the warmest spot. Every evening is a repetition of the previous one, and I start to wonder how long it will take until I feel better.

It takes ten days. They are a scary ten days, waiting for the axe to fall. I am under no illusions about how this germ can go south in the blink of an eye.

Alida asks me a few times whether I want to do a chest x-ray. Just to check. I most certainly do not want to have any kind of x-ray. I do not even want to check my oxygen saturations. Denial is much stronger than I would have thought.

I am initially surprised that I got Covid after such a long time. But, thinking about it, I suppose that it is a numbers game. How much exposure to the virus, and how strong my immunity is at the time of exposure? The week before I got sick, I had an average of five resuscitations a day on Covid positive patients. Even wearing a mask and gloves, the germ had access. And the number of germs is a very important factor.

On the last of the ten days, I feel up to a long walk with the snoopies. Alida and I set off, resting often in pools of cool shade. When we sit down, we notice that they place themselves facing outwards in a circle around us, like the spokes of a wheel. Initially, I put this down to coincidence; but after the third rest we realise that they are strategically positioning themselves to keep guard. We are one of their pack, and they are keeping us in the centre of the circle.

At six the next morning, thinner and greyer but exactly ten days from the Night of the Long Nose Swabs, I am at my post.

Forty-One

1 SEPTEMBER 2021

Spring day and Covid seems to have simply disappeared. I hear on the media that there are still cases, but we are not seeing them in our hospital. The third wave was in full force for almost a hundred days. By mid-August, I could feel it slowing down. Now there is an eerie absence of it. The waiting makes me anxious but it is better than the chaos.

The first wave lasted about seventy-four days, the second around seventy-five days. So, if the pattern holds, we can look forward to four months of chaos towards the end of the year.

A car pulls into the ambulance bay. There is a lady in the passenger seat who looks unresponsive, and we rush out with a stretcher to get her. Luckily, she is breathing on her own, but she is unconscious. We lug her out and wheel her into the resuscitation area. Her daughter hurries alongside, giving us a basic history.

She is eighty-eight years old and previously well. She went on a bus tour to view the Namaqualand daisies ten days ago. She did not come home with the tour bus, and, after extensive searching, her daughter found out that she been left behind in the Western Cape. Apparently, she had not woken up one morning and the tour bus departed without her. She was later found asleep in the hotel room by the manager. They called an ambulance and took her to a tiny clinic in rural Western Cape.

Daisy's daughter eventually located her at the clinic. She was still asleep. The daughter drove down to fetch her and brought her back to Johannesburg. The trip took sixteen hours and Daisy slept the whole way.

Her daughter hands over a letter from the clinic. It seems that they assessed Daisy as being drowsy because she was allergic to the Namaqualand flowers.

I stare at the letter for a few moments. Daisy is not asleep; she is unconscious, and she has probably been unconscious for more than a week. How would an allergy to flowers cause that? It seems that there were no investigations done. I am not sure if they even put up a drip to give her fluids. The fact that she is still alive is a miracle, although she is very dehydrated. Her tongue is like a shriveled, dry leaf in her mouth.

I start with a drip, some blood tests, and a CT scan of her brain. The scan tells me that she has had a massive bleed between her brain and the membrane surrounding it. The membrane is called the dura, I guess because it is tough and durable. This kind of bleed is called sub-dural haematoma. It keeps oozing and creating pressure and the fact that the skull cannot expand, and the brain cannot really be compressed, results in a disastrous situation first recognised and recorded in the year 1783.

I am amazed that this newsflash has not yet reached Namaqualand.

Called the Monro Kelly doctrine, it explains that you cannot add or subtract volume to the inside of the skull without dire consequences. If one of the veins under the dura tears, as has happened with poor Daisy, the blood displaces the cerebrospinal fluid until it reaches a tipping point. This is the point beyond which the CSF is all squeezed out and the brain is pushed down the spinal cord by the oncoming tide of blood. This process can take anything from an hour to a month, depending on the speed of the bleed; but once the brain starts to slip downwards, the pupils fix and dilate and there is nothing that we can do.

Daisy's pupils are still responding to light and so she is a candidate for urgent neurosurgery. Most doctors shine a light into a patient's eyes as a routine examination for head injury. By the time the pupils are behaving abnormally because the brain is damaged, the patient is very seldom conscious. Every child or baby who has had a bump on the head, regardless of whether they are bouncing off the walls or playing on an I-pad, gets the torch shone in their eyes. I do it too. In a conscious patient with no other neurological signs, unequal pupil size or response to light is more likely to be something wrong with the pupil itself, rather than the brain.

Daisy has pretty blue eyes with caramel-coloured flecks, and I check twice that the pupil on the same side and the other side contract when the light blips them. They are working perfectly, and the neurosurgeon accepts her with glee. Sub-dural bleeds are their bread and butter.

Poor Daisy, left for dead on the vibrant carpet of Namaqualand flowers, needs a hole drilled in her skull as soon as possible.

She makes an excellent recovery and I mark her up on my side of the scoreboard against Grim.

Forty-Two

15 November 2021

We have gone for more than 45 days without a Covid case in the ED.

So far, I have not recovered my sense of taste or smell. So much for cooking and eating: they were probably overrated anyway. This pandemic has taken so much from so many people and is still burning bright. Social media is full of eulogies, and everyone knows people who have died from Covid.

I am grateful that I can still see the sunsets, listen to beautiful music, and feel the silky snoopies under my fingertips.

Aside from the lack of taste and smell, the most debilitating thing is that I have developed short-term memory loss. It is most bizarre; a very different feeling to being forgetful. It is like reaching into a totally blank space, where you know that there should be something, but it is resoundingly empty. No thread to tug to bring the garment to light.

There is just nothing.

I have always been adept at holding different things in my mind. It is not really multitasking, but more an adult adaption of an attention deficit disorder. My conscious focus likes to jump between things, and I have always found it easy to run different tasks in parallel and find my place instantly when I hop across. Even as a medical student, I was concurrently studying for a technical diploma in mechanical engineering. I found the variety soothing. Working in the ED suits this habit of shifting focus. I have never had difficulty keeping an eye on my own and other doctors' patients while I work.

After the Covid infection, though, I simply cannot remember things. I will see a patient and send them for an x-ray and, when they reappear, I have absolutely no idea who they are or what test I sent them for. I look at my phone and see that I called the gynaecologist this morning at seven, but I have no idea why.

Today I see my favourite surgeon in the corridor, and he asks me if I have seen the blood results for a patient that I referred.

'What patient?' I ask absently.

'The guy with appendicitis,' he says.

'Appendicitis?' I ask, grasping frantically around in my mind. 'Today?'

I see a glimmer of concern in his eye. 'Yes.' He tells me the guy's name and I still cannot recall anything about him.

Luckily the severe memory loss has only lasted a few weeks and now it is slowly improving. Interestingly, acknowledging it to myself leads me to dying the grey out of my hair for the first time.

I don't want any young puppy doctors thinking that I am over the hill. Although, when you are over the hill, you pick up speed.

Forty-Three

4 December 2021

We are well into the fourth wave. There is a new variant called Omicron, with the emphasis on the oh as in 'oh my goodness'. Omicron is the fifteenth letter of the Greek alphabet, and the variant was first identified in South Africa.

We are all patting our own backs and congratulating each other about our scientific achievement.

The thirteenth letter of the Greek alphabet, nu, was skipped in terms of naming new variants, as was the fourteenth letter xi. Nu sounds too much like 'new', and xi is apparently a very common surname.

As a knee jerk, although Omicron has already been identified worldwide, many countries have banned travel to and from South Africa. This is a tragedy for families who were planning to connect with each other after two long years of famine.

Over the past week, the number of positives had doubled daily. Today just over 11 000 positives in South Africa and, if the numbers in the ED are anything to go by, we will be over 20 000 by Monday. Fuelling the fire, there have been loads of year-end functions and even an attempt at Matric Rage Festival. People feel strongly about their right not to be locked down again. About jib-jabbers and anti-jib-jabbers. About conspiracy theories and possible genocide of an entire older cohort who were denied treatment in some countries. About Big Pharma wanting to control the markets or maybe just kill us all off, which makes no financial sense to me.

   I trudge wearily onward.

Forty-Four

25 December 2021

There is a half-eaten biscuit on the ledge outside my office. It rests on the top of the bumper strip that lines the corridors. Correctly called wall guards, they are there to prevent stretchers colliding with the wall and taking little chunks out of the plaster. I am doing an experiment on how long the biscuit will be allowed to remain there. I photograph it with my mobile from different angles, trying to get the exact feel of abandonment.

This wave is unfolding differently, and I feel a glimmer of hope. Please, I beg the Universe daily, let this virus become attenuated. So far, we are seeing lots of sore throats and headaches; fevers and body aches, but nothing like the severe respiratory cases of the third wave. There are some admissions but not nearly as much oxygen dependence.

I am keeping a personal record of how the vaccinated are faring as compared to the unvaccinated. I am also surprised that some unvaccinated people are still taking Ivermectin, and that many insist on an antibiotic. I explain over and over that Covid is a virus and that it is not treated with an antibiotic. Antibiotics treat bacteria. In fact, it is specifically bad practice to give antibiotics to patients with viral infections. I am always amazed at how much false information is out there and the pandemic seems to have exascerbated the situation.

Everyone is an expert. Which amazes me, because I have been doing this job for a long time and I still don't have a solid grip on this virus. There are so many conspiracy theories, some of which seem quite viable, except I am never sure who 'they' are. A few top lizards, whole governments, economists trying to trim the excess elderly?

Christmas Day seems to attract gynaecology patients to the ED. Special gifts just for me; I almost expect them to have tinsel in their hair. Our hospital does not have an obstetrics and gynaecology department, which makes management from the ED much more difficult. Pregnant patients who are planning to deliver elsewhere, or have already delivered and now have complications, make my job a challenge.

My Christmas present this year is one of the latter. A very personable young woman delivered a healthy baby at another Johannesburg clinic a few days ago. She had some vaginal spotting, which she thought normal, but last night she started to bleed heavily. Today she feels faint, and she passed out at home. She certainly looks a bit green around the gills, and her husband is totally freaked out.

I ask her how many pads she has used so far. What is heavy for one person is not necessarily heavy for another. She tells me that she is wearing an adult diaper – and it is the third one of the day.

This is not a good sign.

We get up a drip and I examine her. She is correct, she is bleeding a lot. In fact, she is bleeding to death right in front of me. Despite the drip full open, she loses consciousness again halfway through the examination. Her blood pressure is unrecordable and she is white as a sheet. I speed dial the gynae and hurriedly give the history.

Long story short, the patient is having a post-partum haemorrhage.

These words are enough to strike fear into the heart of any

gynaecologist. One of the most lethal complications of childbirth, patients with a post-partum haemorrhage can bleed out in a matter of hours. The normal mechanism of the uterine muscles, which chokes off the blood supply of the perforating arteries, does not lock down; the uterus becomes floppy, and the blood simply pours out.

And when I say it is pouring out, that is not an exaggeration. Despite pulling out clots the size of dinner plates, the blood streams out of my patient's vagina like a river.

There is a true moment of panic for me as I wipe and hold and wipe again. The fact that I can't actually see where she is bleeding from makes this even more panic worthy.

'Give Synto,' the gynaecologist advises urgently.

I have already sent a nurse to the pharmacy to get the Syntocinon, which is a drug that makes the uterus contract. While I am waiting for it, I get up another line and start a second litre of fluid. This one is called a colloid, and it is denser than saline or other crystalloids. It should have a better effect on getting her blood pressure up.

Within five minutes I have the Synto, and it is running in. The blood keeps streaming out and I have tilted the bed at 45 degrees head down to try and maintain blood flow to the brain. The lady is still unconscious and now her breathing is becoming irregular.

I am running into trouble here and I dial the gynaecologist again. She confirms that I have given the Synto and cleared any clots from the cervix. Blood clots in the cervix can cause a precipitous drop in blood pressure.

I have done both.

'You must manually stop the bleeding,' she tells me. 'Squash the uterus between your hands. One hand in the vagina firmly on the cervix and the other on the external abdominal wall. Hold it like that until I get there.'

She lives quite far away, but at least there will be no traffic today. I curse under my breath and hold tight. Sweat is pouring off my forehead and joining the ever-increasing pool of blood on the bed. My glasses steam up beneath the mask and plastic visor. Despite double gloves, I am literally up to my elbows in blood.

I am reminded why gynaecology as a specialty was never an attractive option to me. I like to see what I am doing, not trying to fix an invisible thing through a narrow pipe while being drenched from above.

Thank goodness the bleeding seems to be stemming a bit. Head down between her thighs, I keep up the pressure until I hear the gynae's voice in the corridor. By now the bleeding has stopped and the patient is drowsy but awake. Everything seems fine, except for the ten years that I have aged over the past hour.

I really am getting too old for this job.

Once the gynae has carted the post-partum haemorrhage off to ICU, I move along to a lady who is lying like a beached whale on the middle bed in the Covid side.

As I trot from the green to the red side, I see that the biscuit on the wall guard is gone. This is strangely disappointing to me, and I make a mental note to examine my sentiments later. I know that I have separation anxiety, which makes it an enormous struggle to throw away my pen when it runs out of ink, but my attachment to that biscuit was different.

The Whale is moving only her eyes, side to side, looking at her fellow Covids. If obesity is as much of a risk factor as I think it is, she should have been vaccinated. But she was not and it's too late now. She tells me that she is Covid negative. I show her the two stripes on the rapid antigen test. She shakes her head and her multiple chins quiver. She tells me that she has tested every second day and her test is negative. Now she has a fever, a headache and a sore throat.

I explain to her that she has Covid.

'But my test is negative.' She is adamant.

'Your test was negative two days ago, but you had no symptoms, so you should not have been testing anyway. Now you have symptoms, and your test is positive, so you obviously caught it.'

'From where?' Her tone is accusing. I shrug. 'Anywhere, I

guess,' I reply. 'But your oxygen saturations are fine for now and your chest is clear, so it is just symptomatic treatment.'

'What does that mean?' She eyes me warily.

'That we give you medication for your symptoms. Something for pain. Something for nausea. Use it as you need it. When you feel better, you can stop taking it.'

'I need an antibiotic for my cough. It is going to my chest.'

'It is, indeed, going to your chest. But it is a virus. So, there is not much that we can do about it, aside from admit you for oxygen and steroids if you need it. Which, at this point, you don't. But that could change, which is why you have the little finger peg to monitor your oxygen at home.' I try to remove the sing-song-ness from my tone, that tone that one uses for a child under the age of five, but I am not sure that I am successful.

Beached Whale is unhappy.

'I know my own body, doctor, and I am telling you that I need an antibiotic.'

I want to sigh, but I don't want to breath any more Covid than is absolutely necessary. I try to explain the actions of antibiotics again, but she is adamant. A script for an antibiotic is the only reason that she has come to the hospital.

It would be easier to just write the blasted thing and get done. Avoid the inevitable complaint and demand for a refund.

But I won't. It is exactly this contrariness that is somehow my strength and my biggest downfall.

The Whale moves from self-pity to attack mode in a blink.

'You are not a very nice person,' she tells me.

'Probably not,' I answer. 'But my main role here is to help you. Being nice is like the salad on the side.'

I will gladly prescribe a pill to treat stupidity, but, so far, there is no such thing. And if I were to patent one, I would not be working Christmas Day in the ED. I would be swanning around the world on a yacht.

Forty-Five

21 January 2022

Today is the anniversary of the ECMO chopper crash and I am reminded about where we were this time last year. A very rocky ride, to say the least, but there is a trace of hope that somehow the world will return to some form of sanity. Covid patients are still rolling in, but it is more like a calm day at the beach than the tsunami that it was. The waves and ripples feel more predictable, the ebb and flow of the tide less freakish.

A couple is waiting in room three. They have angelic faces, like fragile China dolls with striking blue eyes and wispy haloes of hair. They are concerned because the husband is not feeling well and collapsed on his way to the bathroom this morning. He seemed to be breathing strangely, the wife reports.

He is sitting on the bed, reading a book He looks comfortable, even though the novel is a Stephen King. The patient does not seem short of breath at first glance, but I see that his oxygen saturations are hovering around 80 per cent, which is too low for a healthy young man.

I pick up his hand to check that the probe – which is like a velvety clothes peg – is property seated on his fingertip.

To my alarm, his nail beds are all navy blue.

'Do your fingernails always look like this?' I ask him.

'They started looking like that last night,' his wife replies. 'Maybe he is cold.'

I hold his hands in mine and they are not cold. Maybe the Steven King novel is more frightening to him than it seems. Clowns materialising out of plug holes and holding bouquets of balloons terrorised me as a child.

'Huh,' I say and unloop my stethoscope from around my neck. His chest is clear.

'Any cough or chest pain?' I enquire.

'Nope,' he replies and puts his book aside. I press on his fingernails and release them to see if the capillaries refill. They remain the same.

I learned about dusky or blue fingernails at medical school. Called peripheral cyanosis, it shows very poor oxygenation. I have seen it in older, heavy smokers but nothing like this in an otherwise well young person. It is very concerning. It is also strange that he is not breathing fast, and that he seems so unconcerned.

I ask him if he has tested for Covid.

He has had Covid twice; both documented with clear positive tests at the lab and suitable symptoms. I ask for some blood tests, an ECG and a chest x-ray. I hook him up to oxygen and the monitor makes a happier tone.

Navy Nails reverts to his novel, and his wife to her phone.

I hover around, trying not to look too concerned, and see other patients while I wait for his blood and x-ray results. A single candle burns in the corridor in memory of the ECMO team. It seems a lifetime ago.

One of the blood tests that I request for Navy Nails is called a d-dimer. It looks for fragments of clot and the level should be less than 0.5. Navy Nails has a d-dimer greater than ten. I scoot him downstairs for a CT angiogram. The images confirm a massive clot in his pulmonary artery. Called a saddle embolism, it straddles both main branches and usually the affected patient collapses and dies within minutes.

I call my favourite physician and discover that he has a locum for the weekend. The only good thing about that is a new number for my database. I enter his name and number in my mobile and then call him. I tell him about Navy Nails – his episode of fainting, the fact that he is stable now aside from the cyanosis. Oh yes, and the low saturations.

'Perhaps you should do a dimer?' he suggests.

'Yep, did that, it is greater than ten.'

'Ten!' He sounds alarmed. 'Well, then he needs a CT angiogram.'

'Yep, did that, shows a saddle embolism.'

'*What*?' This poor locum, it is his first patient on his first day covering a private casualty.

'Oh dear, I will be there shortly.'

'Shall I start him on anticoagulant?'

'Yes, yes…' He sounds flustered.

The Locum trots into the ED within a few minutes. We greet each other and I like him immediately. He fits the physician profile perfectly: sincere, thoughtful, hardworking. Physicians can err on the side of being arrogant, given the depth and breadth of their training and that they are often called to the patient after the easy-to-make mistakes have been made, and they often consider themselves cleverer than the norm. But this doctor is not one of those.

He gets a full history and examines Navy Nails. The nailbeds are slightly less blue than they were on arrival, mostly because I have put him on oxygen, but I can't really switch off the oxygen to maximise their effect for the Locum.

When the Locum sees the CT angiogram, he sits down on the desk and shakes his head. 'How is this guy even still alive?' he mutters. My thoughts exactly. I have already given an injection under the skin to thin Navy's blood, but the question is whether we should go full tilt and give him an intravenous blood thinner.

Locum is on the horn to my favourite physician immediately. Together, they decide to give a half dose of the intravenous blood thinner. I have read some articles on this, and I feel that it is the correct decision. The Locum takes my notes from the desk and heads for the door.

'Um, sorry, those are my notes,' I tell him.

'Oh,' he says. 'I thought that they go with the patient.'

'No. That is how it works in government hospitals, but in private you all write your own notes.' He looks so crestfallen that I make him a copy of my notes and give him a blank sheet of paper from the photocopier. I even slap a sticker with Navy's details on the top.

'But how is there any continuity of care if everyone writes their own notes?' The Locum is bemused.

'Continuity of care?' I echo. What a lovely phrase. 'I suppose we talk to each other on the phone.' I think back to my days training in government. Each patient had a file which was called the bed letter. Every ward round, instruction, postulation and test result was meticulously recorded in the bed letter. It was golden. Now we have everything on a computer or an app.

I stand at the memorial candle for a few moments and stare at the blurry photograph of the ECMO team. A jumble of thoughts and feelings are just outside my reach, but at least I feel less dead inside than I did last year.

I even have energy to prowl the hospital.

There is an elderly lady standing at the lift. She has not pressed the button and I wonder if it is Covid avoidance. I am sure the button is teeming with germs, but I push it anyway. With a ping, the lift arrives and door sighs open. We step in and she grasps my forearm.

'I am terrified of lifts,' she whispers urgently.

I wonder why she didn't take the stairs, but I guess that she is over eighty and they may be too much for her.

'Don't worry. I'm a doctor,' I tell her. I am amazed at the words as they are spoken, and they hang awkwardly in the closed space. In thirty years, I have never used that phrase; and here it is, splendidly redundant. Doctor or not, if the mechanism breaks, we will both plummet to our death.

No 'out loud' voice, I remind myself.

'Oh, thank goodness,' she says, her eyes locking on mine. She still has my forearm in a vice-grip. At least she looks soothed, no matter how irrational it is. I watch the floors click by until we reach hers and she shuffles out with another grateful 'thank you' over her shoulder.

At least I was of some assistance. Before Covid, the medical profession felt powerful. We had whispered spells that wove a strong magic. We had tinctures and tricks and genuinely well-thought-out strategies. For the last two years we have been screaming into the wind, watching helplessly as our patients are decimated despite our best efforts.

We lost heart. We lost our confidence. But it feels like the tide may be turning now.

Perhaps, as my mother always said, fortune favours the brave.